D0897622

New myths and old realities; [college
counseling in transition, by] Charles F.
Warnath.   San Francisco, Jossey-Bass,
1971.
    xiv, 172 p. (The Jossey-Bass series in
higher education)

    1. Personnel service in higher educa-
tion. I. Warnath, Charles F.

New Myths
and
Old Realities

College Counseling
in Transition

Charles F. Warnath

NEW MYTHS
AND
OLD REALITIES

Jossey-Bass Inc., Publishers
San Francisco · Washington · London · 1971

NEW MYTHS AND OLD REALITIES
College Counseling in Transition
by Charles F. Warnath

Copyright © 1971 by Jossey-Bass, Inc., Publishers

Published in Great Britain by
Jossey-Bass, Inc., Publishers
St. George's House
44 Hatton Garden, London E.C.1

Library of Congress Catalogue Card Number LC 77-172879

International Standard Book Number ISBN 0-87589-114-4

Manufactured in the United States of America

JACKET DESIGN BY WILLI BAUM

FIRST EDITION

Code 7134

The Jossey-Bass
Series in Higher Education

Consulting Editor

HAROLD L. HODGKINSON
University of California, Berkeley

The Jossey-Bass
Series in Higher Education

Preface

This is a very personal book. Those friends and colleagues with whom I have agreed as well as those with whom I have had differences of opinions over the years will recognize familiar themes. I have cited relatively few journal article and book sources and may, thus, stand accused of lacking academic rigor. This omission was not purposeful but simply due to the fact that little of significance has been written about the settings in which professional counseling is offered. Professional counseling has a considerable literature, but, with few exceptions, it is theoretical and ideal; the research reported in journals is valuable primarily as it accords its authors academic credits and professional status among other academicians.

My book is essentially the product of my sixteen years in three college counseling centers, the last ten as the director at Oregon State. I have worked with clients long enough to understand my potential for bias, distortion, and projection. However, my purpose is not to reveal "truth" but to raise questions, stir up discussion, and rock a few comfortable boats within the profession.

I have, in one sense, been working on the manuscript since my

ix

first year as a college counselor. Three events shattered my expectations of carrying out my professional duties entirely within the confines of the counseling room and made me question my adequacy as a college counselor. First, I managed a preregistration orientation week for freshman students. Second, I inadvertently annoyed the mother of a senior student from a small, isolated community who called the chancellor to object to my comments to the graduating class on the unsuitability of a university education for some of them. And, finally, our counseling center staff became embroiled with the dean of students over his demand for access to the counseling files. This incident resulted in the resignation of the entire full-time staff. By then it was clear to me that a counselor must be concerned with much more than interactions with his clients if he is to survive in an institutional setting. Nothing has happened to me since to change my mind.

Several years ago, the directors of college counseling centers, at their annual meeting, decided on a much-needed publication on the activities of college counseling centers, and I undertook the task. The material in this book is the result of that stimulus, and, although it is not an official presentation by any particular group or organization, its content is due in large measure to suggestions made by a number of directors. The problems and issues presented have been discussed with many counselors and directors.

Although it is difficult to single out particular people who have contributed to my thinking, I do wish to thank Thomas Magoon of the University of Maryland, David Danskin of Kansas State University, and Sumner Morris of the University of California, Davis, as early encouragers of the project; Theodore Volsky of the University of Colorado, whose radical questioning of the value of traditionally trained counseling psychologists in the college setting confirmed many of my ideas; and Harry Sharp of the University of Wyoming and Donald Hartsough of Purdue, who read and criticized early drafts of the manuscript. My special thanks to David Danskin and to Sheridan McCabe of the University of Notre Dame for many of the ideas which appear in my final chapter, and also, of course,

Preface

special thanks to the many colleagues who have suffered through my frustrations and annoyances. These people, in a sense, have written the book.

The book is aimed at three groups: graduate students preparing to enter professional counseling in an institutional setting; graduate faculties in counselor education programs who need to become more aware than they now are of professional problems in institutional and organizational settings; and staffs of counseling services, who often view their problems and difficulties as unique and vent their feelings of frustration and anger on each other. I also hope that institutional administrators, particularly those in and preparing for student personnel posts, will read my book. Because counseling centers tend to be assigned, for administrative purposes, to the student personnel area, there is considerable misunderstanding when the counselors behave like professional counselors, whose primary focus is the clients they serve, rather than like administrators, whose primary job focus tends to be the institutional structure and procedures.

I have tried to draw the framework (both organizationally and attitudinally) within which professional counselors generally operate. The picture may seem rather bleak. It may discourage some graduate students who are looking forward to working in a service agency within an institutional setting. The impression of struggle and frustration has been intentional. My purpose is to offset the rosy glow of idealism which those preparing to enter the profession seem to receive during their graduate education. I hope that if some of the problems are discussed openly and honestly prior to the acceptance of a position by a new counselor in a service agency, his shock upon arrival will be diminished, and he will not take out his feelings of upended expectations on his colleagues.

If I am able to stir up some genuine confrontation within our profession, I will have accomplished my purpose. At present we talk to each other in our books and journals about the horsepower of our engine but very little about where we are going or why we are making the trip. We have certainly ignored the conditions of

Preface

the road and the attitudes of those who are paying the expenses. Many more forces work on the counselor than the adequacy with which he carries out his procedures in the counseling session.

Corvallis, Oregon   CHARLES F. WARNATH
September 1971

Contents

Contents

New Myths
and
Old Realities

*College Counseling
in Transition*

Problems of College Counseling

ONE

In the early 1950s a Division of Counseling was established within the American Psychological Association (APA) and the first *Journal of Counseling Psychology* was published. The literature in counseling has expanded steadily since then—written for those self-consciously engaged in developing a profession.

With their professional organization, their journal, and an extensive literature, the expectation might be that professional counselors of the 1970s would be confident about their activities and engaged in building upon a firm foundation of theory and practice. Quite the opposite is true. Counseling psychologists (and other pro-

1

fessional counselors) continue in the throes of an identity crisis. The issue of clinical versus counseling practice is still being debated. A simmering disagreement over the roles of the professional counselor has erupted anew. But who could expect a profession to stabilize itself on an activity inherent in a variety of human relationships? We may have been responsible for refining the activity but we have been unable to define the conditions and situations in which that activity must be the exclusive possession of our professional group.

Ours is a bloodless profession in the sense that, like the experimental psychologists' subjects, the clients of the counseling literature exist apart from their communities; their counselors work in settings untroubled by human relationship and organizational pressures which affect other working people. Who asks what Jim of Seeman's interview transcriptions of *The Case of Jim* (1957) was sacrificing to pay the fee for his eighty or more therapy sessions, or what type of institutional setting permits that investment of time in one person? We are satisfied to learn how a sensitive, client-centered therapist interacts with a client in trouble.

Who asks how Carl Rogers' concepts of counseling and the blurring of lines between counseling and psychotherapy have been affected by the institutional settings in which he has worked? In several articles Patterson (1968, 1968a, 1969b), a practicing Rogerian, has defined the work of the counselor in a way which would restrict the counselor to serving a relatively small clientele in individual contacts—an elite of the sick. Patterson rejects any role for the college counselor but that of a psychotherapist engaged in individual contacts of indeterminate length. Has he had to defend his point of view with a dean of students, a taxpayers' group, or the students on a counseling center waiting list? But Patterson's view, divorced from the service settings in which a majority of counselors practice their art, is not unusual in the counseling literature. With such stuff are myths created and perpetuated; and mythology provides a poor base for a creative and developing service profession. The community supports only those services which it perceives as of value and significance to itself.

The professional counselor finds himself in a dilemma—he

can risk either the loss of his position by ignoring the expectations of his supporting community or the loss of his professional identity by disregarding the mythology of his profession (gained by his training and literature), which measures his worth by a standard of individual counseling. Patterson's myth is harmful to development of the profession—a profession defined in terms more appropriately of attitudes of service than of technique.

The counseling psychologist, as noted by Shoben (1958), has grown up within the tradition of American higher education. Samler's analysis of the settings in which counseling psychologists were employed in 1963 revealed that 62 per cent of his sample of APA members were working in colleges and universities (1964). The development and current problems of counseling within higher education affect large numbers of professional counselors. The counselor's role cannot be appreciated without an understanding of his working environment. To know only what occurs between client and counselor within the counseling cubicle is to totally ignore that both the client and the counselor are people engaged in life struggles apart from their one-hour-per-week contacts; both operate within social and institutional frameworks beyond the direct control of either which strongly affect their critical, but nonetheless fleeting, confrontations.

Current activities of college counseling centers can be seen in clearer perspective by outlining their historical development. The early form of most organizations lays the foundation of expectations within the community and establishes patterns of personnel replacements and support which determine to a greater or lesser degree what the later form of that organization is likely to be. With few exceptions, colleges had no professional counselors on campus until the Veterans Administration established guidance bureaus following World War II. The colleges were required to invest little of their own funds. The standards for counselors were minimal. The procedures were routine. A veteran needed the approval of a V.A. counselor for his initial program and any later significant change. The guidance bureau, therefore, was primarily a placement and educational monitoring device to protect the government investment in

3

G.I. subsidies. Those who assumed the directorship of a center at a four-year institution which had its origins in the V.A. were confronted by file cases of dusty folders containing almost identical batteries of tests, official forms with the familiar boxes for checking, and monotonously similar, scribbled comments and evaluations. Counselors had often been civil service personnel from welfare, employment, or armed services offices who apparently wanted (or were encouraged) to take a tour of duty on the campus; or they were graduate students enrolled in a practicum or internship for a degree in guidance. The director may have been an excaptain with a personnel specialty, or he may have been an absentee department chairman with little involvement in the center activities other than signing forms and reports.

This is the picture of the college counseling center which the deans, business managers, and presidents currently making priority decisions about the counseling center received while attending college or, perhaps, acting as guidance personnel themselves. It is quite different from the abstractions which the present graduate school professors convey to their trainees. Thus the expectations of college personnel for counseling centers were established five to ten years prior to the formation of a professional organization for those who considered themselves the standard setters for professional counseling.

Finally the number of veterans diminished and the V.A. phased out its guidance bureaus. Some colleges, however, assumed budget responsibilities for such centers; it was at this point that college counseling split along several lines. These were logical, but none were more than minimally related to professional considerations. College activities (like courses) are often perpetuated more for what they do for the administrators and faculty than what they do for students. Thus, most centers were extensions or modifications of the guidance bureaus rather than being thoughtfully modeled on theoretical and professional lines.

Where practicum students and interns had been serving as counselors, the center often became the captive center of a psychology department, and the clinical and counseling faculty applied for training grants to replace their guidance bureau support. What the new arrangement would do for the students on campus seemed less important than what it would do for the facilities and personnel of the department. Where an appropriate psychology staff did not exist, the center might become a centralized advising center, staffed by junior faculty who generally continued the interview-test interpretation format established by the guidance bureaus.

The routine was sometimes disrupted by the arrival of a junior faculty member on the staff who had taken a few clinical psychology courses. The campus was then jolted temporarily into awareness of the center when word got around that it was especially encouraging the application of coeds with sexual problems. On a campus with a conservative administration this activity could obviously be detrimental to the growth of a sound counseling program, but this is one example of the manner in which personal and political factors have sometimes affected the application of theoretical and abstract concepts about counseling at the point of delivery.

A high proportion of the centers were assigned to whatever administrator was considered responsible for the student activities and services. In the early 1950s this person was perhaps a senior faculty member who had been passed over for a deanship within his area, a former military officer, or a faculty member who had lost his zest for research within his discipline. The size, staffing, and focus of the center were largely determined by who, at that point, happened to be the chief staff member and his personal and status relationships with the administration. Professional counseling considerations were secondary. Other centers were assigned, for administrative convenience, to some department, school, or an academic dean, one chip in the ongoing political game of power and influence on campus. There is no discernible inherent pattern—certainly none influenced by the profession. The birth of the counseling center was unplanned, springing as it did from the influences of local institutions rather than from theories of counseling, educational philosophy, or the needs of a particular student body.

Directors in those early days were faculty or administrators with other responsibilities: testing or personnel research coordinators, directors of freshman orientation and advising programs, and instructors or supervisors of guidance programs. In some cases the directors, as in the V.A. period, were absentee coordinators; they maintained contact with the center primarily through reports from the junior faculty and graduate students who carried on the service contacts with the undergraduate clientele. The variety of directors and their personal role and status within campus communities produced a range of center styles. However, except in some of those centers used as clinical internship facilities (captive centers), the core service remained in educational-vocational guidance with an emphasis on testing. This emphasis was predictable not only because the guidance bureaus had established a set of expectations for the services of counseling centers, but also because the early centers were organized before professional leaders had made any attempts to establish standards and guidelines.

The first conference of professional leaders was not until 1951. The Northwestern Conference is described by Robinson (1964) as having "worked on standards for Ph.D. training to provide for the first time a broad and unified view of our field." 1951 was also the year of the first meeting of counseling directors, when almost fifty, primarily from the Midwest, met to share problems. Not until 1953 did the leadership drop *Guidance* from the title of our division of the APA. Almost no direction came from the profession during the first decade in which the colleges assumed responsibility for the operation of counseling centers. The situation has improved very little and, if anything, the gap has widened between the counselor's academic training and the realities of the service agencies which hire the new graduates—but more on that later.

That some institutions are more adaptable to counseling services than others is often overlooked in evaluating the current status of college counseling centers. Without doubt, the midwestern land grant college proved most successful in incorporating a counseling center into its organizational structure. With its practical applied programs in the fields of engineering, agriculture, business, and home economics and a student population of middle-class young people from predominantly unsophisticated rural areas, the midwestern land grant college could view the educational-vocational guidance aspects of a counseling center as an asset to its educational advising program. Upwardly mobile young people with limited experiences needed assistance in making decisions about their future. The liberal arts colleges in the main have ignored "professional counseling" until recently, with the exception of those schools where the department of psychology or the school of education has subsidized a captive center for practicum training. Public colleges and universities have generally been receptive to counseling which their administrators perceive as educational-vocational assistance, while the less vocationally oriented, private liberal arts colleges and universities have invested in clinical-psychiatric service to care for the personal-emotional problems of their students.

It is not by chance that E. G. Williamson became an early spokesman for a directive advising style of counseling from his base at the University of Minnesota, while Rogers developed a system of counseling without external goals in the liberal arts atmosphere of The University of Chicago. Further evidence of this differentiation is seen in the extensive counseling center operations of the Big Ten Schools, which have provided a substantial proportion of service and research-oriented counseling personnel throughout the country, while Harvard is best known for its very large psychiatric clinic. The environment and institutional press exert a tremendous influence on the service of the resident practitioners. An institution of higher education tolerates services generally restricted to the affluent as long as those services are supported by other than the general fund (federal grant money, for instance). It does not subsidize services for individuals or an organization (such as a counseling center) unless its administration (or that part which controls the purse strings) is persuaded that the service is directly advantageous to that particular institution and a substantial number of its constituents. Service personnel do not generally realize that they may be valued more for the public relations role which they play for the institution than for their services for students. Harvard, for example, can support a large staff of psychiatrists because psychiatric service is part of the perceptual world of the affluent and knowledgeable parents of its students as well as that of its board of national leaders. If these adults have a personal problem, they probably seek out and are willing to pay for expensive psychiatric services—should they expect less for their children? But the parents of the children from Broken Bow, Nebraska; Fossil, Oregon; or Cutbank, Montana, typically have little understanding of psychotherapy, and most can be persuaded that counseling is a legitimate, tax-supported service only insofar as it helps their young people make specific decisions. When the center can fully cope with basic demands for guidance in decision making, some of its staff can become involved in other activities, including psychotherapy. Nevertheless, one-to-one psychotherapy is, perhaps, the most difficult activity to justify as a tax-supported service in a public college. The marginal farmer, the widowed typist, and the grocery clerk can hardly be enthusiastic about subsidizing the therapy of a student whom they probably consider advantaged simply by his being able to attend college.

Extended clinical work with individual clients, the basis of many texts used in counselor training programs and reinforced in counselor practicums, cannot generally be supported by public colleges and universities with general fund money. The development of counseling services on the college campus has been impeded by much of the counseling literature, written by administrators and staff of the largest and most affluent clincal centers and by faculty of counselor training programs whose centers serve as captive agencies. In the large captive center there is freedom for specialization, difficult in the typical service agency with its relatively small professional staff. In a training center the ties to campus are often tenuous and service to the student body may be of only passing concern. As long as a sufficient number of clients show up to give the trainees adequate experience, the professionals are satisfied that the agency is operating effectively. Those agencies can afford to permit staff considerable clinical activity without the pressure of load accountability. Moreover, the staff in the training centers are usually rewarded by the academic system of the faculty with its emphasis on publication, thus reducing greatly the importance of service productivity. The typical center is constantly trying to meet the service demands of students with an inadequate number of staff and often inadequate facilities. It is therefore logical that counselors within service agencies have begun to utilize more unorthodox methods in their role as psychologists for meeting the needs of the campus.

Professional counselors do not occupy a precise and unambiguous role on the college campus. The term *counseling* has a wide range of meanings throughout the institution. At its lowest common denominator—the most widely held definition by faculty, administrators, and students—counseling is perceived as any face-to-face contact between any adult and any student in the institution, or between one student who is older or has some special information or both and any other student who needs that information. By this common criterion, counseling centers exist in an environment in which almost every adult sees himself, at one time or another, counseling with students and where large numbers of older students are designated as counselors. Faculty, in particular, recognize little difference between their advising activities and the individual student contacts of the professional counselors. The same attitude has been true of other student personnel staff—an attitude given legitimacy by Williamson (1961) in a book for students' personnel administrators. A few years ago, on one campus I found no fewer than six different groups of counselors listed in the student and faculty handbooks. An article in a college newspaper about a tutorial service offered by upper division students for other students who needed academic assistance was headlined: "Counselors to Assist with Academic Problems." Individual counseling gives the professional staff of the center no uniqueness upon which to build a campus identity.

Professional counselors adapt to this ambiguity; however, they pay a psychological price for having no distinct working role within their institution. Their anxiety expresses itself in hostility toward administrative regulations, a protectiveness toward each other's activities, and a sensitivity toward any perceived lack of interest in their work by others in the campus community. However, no matter how well they adjust psychologically to the ambiguity of their position on campus, the counseling center staff are continually

9

in financial competition with other personnel services. At one college the administrative officer responsible for allocating funds for student services equates the work of the undergraduate advisors in the residence halls with that of the counselors in the center. Since the former outnumber the latter about ten to one and cost considerably less, the financial officer sees it as simply good business to divert resources from the center to support the cheaper product.

Outside funds and grants for research, training, and testing permit split appointments with departments and the support of practicum students and interns. These additional personnel give some centers the surface appearance of thriving organizations. Nevertheless, surveys by Warnath (1970) and Magoon (1970) reveal that in colleges and universities with student populations between ten and twenty thousand, the usual number of doctoral-level staff is about three to five and, for colleges under ten thousand, fewer than three. Only thirteen of Magoon's eighty-nine colleges over ten thousand employ ten or more doctoral-level staff in their centers to provide educational-vocational and personal counseling. Very few institutions of higher education support completely adequate counseling center services with general fund money. The largest counseling centers are those where a director or prominent staff member has implemented institutional resources with some nonuniversity funds (such as a statewide testing service or federal training grant).

The budget of the center determines the extent of the staff's activities and most directly affects its individual counseling. A staff member has a limited number of hours available for his service activities; the smaller the staff, the fewer the contact hours available for individual counseling. The higher the average number of contacts devoted to clients, the smaller the number of students who can receive service from the center. Choices must be made, and these are only partly determined by the staff. They are minimally affected by the counseling literature, which tends to assume ideal conditions and a closed system involving only a willing counselor and a motivated client. A counselor presented with a personal-emotional problem is immediately placed in a quandary at most service centers.

Few whose primary responsibility is service rather than training can afford to invest more than one or two hours per week for the equivalent of a term in any one student. The counselor may judge that a student needs a warm relationship over an extended period of time, but that counselor is then confronted with the alternatives of assisting one student, which will involve many hours, or of helping several students who could gain equal benefits from a smaller investment of his time.

This issue is a constant source of conflict for service agency counselors and may explain the anxiety with which many approach individual counseling. Patterson, in the writings cited above, has speculated that counselors are abandoning individual counseling for a variety of ill-considered reasons. There is little evidence to suport his "abandonment" charge, and for those who work under the constant pressure of service agency waiting lists, Patterson's speculations appear academically remote. The professional counselor in the service agency is caught amidst a variety of conflicting institutional pressures. He needs understanding and assistance in coping with these forces from the leaders of his profession—not reasons to feel guilty about the method he is using to resolve the conflicts in his service role.

What should the college counseling center try to accomplish? The implications of professional counseling are rarely discussed in the college community; and the profession states the role of the counselor in idealized terms: a facilitator of individual growth, an aid in decision making, a repository of unconditional positive regard. These commendable traits are attributed to the professional counselor within the closed system of the counselor-client interview. On a grander scale, Williamson (1961) contends that counseling is designed to individualize mass education and to personalize services. But Williamson so dilutes the term that professional counselors simply blend into the total student personnel group along with financial aid officers, residence hall directors, and deans. He minimizes the professional counselor's special contribution to the campus. Through assigning counseling as a generic component to all student personnel services, he seems primarily concerned with giving some

11

sort of coherence to a disparate collection of administrative officials.

Mueller (1961) does no better, spreading counseling through all administrative offices and devoting only one page of her entire book to the counseling center. And, significantly, in *The Counseling of College Students,* not one chapter was written by a staff member or director of a college counseling center (Siegel, 1968). Authors of books and articles for student personnel administrators have hardly clarified the implications of the functions carried on by professional counselors. If anything, they have succeeded merely in emasculating the term and removing it from any serious discussion of institutional goals and purposes. Financial aid officers counsel students into the most appropriate loan and scholarship packages; housing directors counsel students into proper housing; deans counsel students into appropriate extracurricular activities or correct interpretations of the rules. The only question in the mind of the layman is "what do the counselors of the counseling center counsel students into?"

The view of the professional counselors' work by the majority of faculty, students and nonpersonnel administrators leaves the professional counseling staff without significant activity or procedure for which they can claim unique responsibility as contributors to the college community. The professional counselor could formerly console himself by perusing the counseling literatures, which assured him that he was helping students cope with their environment and thus was salvaging young people who might ordinarily be lost to higher education without his intervention. But, given the situation in higher education, this assurance has about the same value as encouraging a couple to produce a houseful of children in an overpopulated world. College campuses have been inundated with students. Faculty, searching for ways to reduce the heavy pressure on their courses, are not enthusiastic about methods designed to retain more students in the institution. Individual counseling has, therefore, become counterproductive to the wishes of many of the staff.

The retention function of the counseling center has also lost some of its meaning for the students. Until recently, the opportunities for a college education were limited; failure in or disappointment

12

with one's chosen college generally meant that a student had no chance of obtaining a college degree. The proliferation of state colleges, community and junior colleges, and other post-high school institutions allows young people a range of possibilities for post-high school education. The increased number of post-high school institutions gives the student a chance to make a new start or remedy failures in a different evironment. At many junior and community colleges, the counseling staff, under these circumstances, become heavily involved in academic advising; thus, in some colleges, the unique role of the professional counselor has all but disappeared.

With proliferation of post-high school opportunities, the mobility of college students is increased. Many students now engage in a cafeteria-style college education, enrolling in one school and transferring to several others before completing degree requirements. Students often spread their college education over five, six, or seven years with vacations between matriculation and commencement for work, travel, or some other nonclassroom experience. For these students, educational-vocational counseling related to the local curriculum is only minimally appropriate. The mobility of students no longer gives the professional counselor justification for support in helping students make wise moves within the curriculum of the institution.

Educational-vocational decision making in the traditional manner is being challenged from many angles. The number of contacts per client in the typical counseling center has averaged slightly more than two, indicating that much professional educational-vocational counseling has been a form of test interpretation processing. Current developmental and self-concept theories raise serious questions about the appropriateness of a method which is essentially a trait-and-factor approach in helping college-age youth with vocational selection. It is, however, the placement features inherent in this testing method of decision making which make the counselor suspect among many college youth. While young people are attacking establishment values, the vocational counselor becomes part of the business-industrial sorting process. Rather than being perceived as concerned primarily with problems of identity and alienation—

13

the immediate concerns of college-age youth—vocational counselors are identified with those adults who want to reaffirm the values of the status quo. Without the confidence of those whom he hopes to help, the professional counselor's effectiveness in the institution is seriously affected.

Until recently, professional counselors have taken for granted their general competence to work with the full range of college students. The arrival of minority students has shaken their confidence. The minority student has pointedly avoided the center. Where the minority group has grown large enough, it has often developed its own assistance programs or demanded the hiring of a counselor from its own ethnic group. Blacks particularly have insisted that the center counselors, coming from white middle-class society, selected and trained in the intellectual-verbal tradition of the middle class, and imbued with white society's traditional values, cannot possibly communicate with young blacks. These charges are not dismissed easily, for the differences in language and outlook become readily apparent after a short conversation with a young person from one of the minority groups.

These problems question the counselor's understanding of other young people with background and orientation different from his own. He has previously been able to protect himself, when clients have not returned after an initial interview, with a rationalization of the client's lack of motivation; now he must face the possibility that the fault lies in his own blind spots, lack of empathy, or unquestioning acceptance of the values of the system within which he is working (Halleck, 1971).

In summary, the college counseling center is in difficulty if it maintains its traditional role on campus as the exclusive agency for individual counseling. Historically, the center in the four-year college developed out of the guidance bureaus established after World War II and with some modification, has continued to offer educational-vocational and personal counseling to individual students as its primary contribution to the campus and to higher education. Changes in the size and composition of the student body have reduced the impact of the center on almost every campus. Shifting attitudes of faculty toward the retention of marginal or confused students and students' suspicions about the identification of the center with the adult society's values make the position of the center in the college community very tenuous. The college counselor is a marginal man. Professional counselors in the centers of numerous colleges are reassessing their roles. They have no other choice.

Myths and Realities

TWO

One counseling center director has said: "We tell each other lies." Enquiring further about specific activities reported by counselors in informal discussions, he discovered that counselors are not always as candid with each other as they might be. They seem to need to exaggerate their independence and the centrality of their role on campus. Very little literature describes or compares the activities of college counseling centers. General outlines of counseling on the college campus have been presented in the writings of student personnel administrators such as Williamson (1961) and Mueller (1961) and in the survey of student services by Gallagher and Demos (1970). A relatively few descriptions of discrete center activities have appeared in the journals (Shoben, 1956; Koile, 1960; Warman, 1961; Clark, 1966; Sinnett and Danskin, 1967; Albert,

16

1968). But for much of our information about the operation of counseling centers, we have had to rely on our informal reports to each other. Only in 1971 was a proposed set of guidelines for college counseling centers, sponsored by a group of directors, published (Kirk, 1971).

Counseling literature, as a projector of the myth of an independent agency, gives the counselor a belief that activities within the agency, seen in isolation and not within the larger environment of the campus community, are self-justified. Because he is perpetuating a myth, he will tell lies to his colleagues, giving the impression that his agency plays a central role on campus. Thus the reasoning become circular. Discrepancies between myth and reality, apart from decreasing the relevance of counselor education programs for the work of practicing counselors, are serious contributors to the counselor's self-doubts and frustrations, and the shock and cynicism among new professionals.

As with other professional groups, the mythology of the counseling profession covers a variety of beliefs related to the practice of members of the group, the members' interactions with other professionals, and the group's organizational and institutional identifications (Bisno, 1960). Through comparative descriptions of the varied activities of counseling agencies, the potential negative influences of this myth on the profession and training of counselors can be seen in perspective.

I have drawn descriptive and comparative data from visits, in 1967, to centers on fourteen campuses. With the exception of one medium-size, private university, all schools are public colleges with enrollments exceeding ten thousand. They are located in communities of various sizes along the West Coast and through the Southwest and Southeast. No typical center exists. There are, however, several basic types of centers with in-group similarities. The basic types differ from each other in the priorities they assign to potential center activities. To view centers as either essentially alike or as different as the number of colleges they serve obscures the commonalities and differences. This view, in turn, perpetuates the counseling myth by permitting the faculty of training programs to persist in the illusion

17

that individual counseling proficiency and some research techniques are the only skills required for the complete counselor. Observation of the functioning of a range of centers illuminates the superficiality of this perception.

The setting in which the personnel perform their duties and the condition of their facilities are often good indicators of the relationship of a unit to the total organization. Within business, the symbols of personal status are well known: use of the executive washroom, size of desk, number of windows, presence of a rug. The symbols of academic hierarchy are more elusive than these, perhaps because the resources available to institutions of higher education have not permitted individuals to flaunt the usual symbols of affluence and power. Status in academic institutions is evident even to those not in the academic community through the location, size, and relative newness of the facilities of various departments and schools. On one campus, a department reputed to be the most powerful group in the institution occupies a modern building of impressive size while the equivalent department on another campus, still struggling to earn approval for a graduate program, occupies the top floor of an ancient, four-story structure.

What have the symbols of academic status to do with the myth of college counseling? The mythical independent center, based on the independent practitioner model, has as its distinctive supporting symbol the central ground-level location on campus free from obvious identifications with teaching and administrative units. To be effective, so counselors tell each other, a center should be accessible to the main student traffic patterns while having no visible connections to potential sources of evaluation and administrative decision-making. But the reality of our situation more often than not differs as much from the mythical ideal as Dick and Jane's family life differs from that of the ordinary American family. In reality the center is probably located on the edge of campus or on the third floor of a crumbling building already abandoned by several prestigeful departments, or perhaps it shares a common entrance with student personnel offices—a far cry from the ideal location touted as necessary for optimum effectiveness.

Myths and Realities

Of the fourteen counseling centers, only one is housed in a separate building, and this center, significantly, is a large federally assisted training facility. Another is on the third floor of a student activities center, with no indication on the first floor of its presence in the building. Five are located in buildings clearly designated as administration, four others are in undesignated office buildings containing administrative offices, one is in a combination classroom-administration building, and two are in academic buildings. Excluding the center located in a separate building, only two of the fourteen centers have ground-level locations.

Factors other than accessibility to student traffic patterns and isolation from evaluative and administrative sources appear to have determined the location of these centers. The main factors which seem to determine the location of these centers are chance and the decisions of administrators unaffiliated with the center. The center is usually located where minimally adequate space becomes available. As confirmed by McLean's survey (1967), a college counseling center is often a tenant in space controlled by some other academic or administrative division. Whether it loses effectiveness through these associations is a moot point.

The college counseling center is also not the private preserve of the counseling psychologist. Only half of the centers surveyed are directed by counseling psychologists. A psychiatrist, a client-centered therapist, two clinicians, two vocational guidance specialists, and a professional from a field unrelated to psychology administer the affairs of the other seven centers. The duties of these directors are as varied as their specialties. As indicated in figures obtained from a nationwide sample of directors by Oetting (1970), the proportion of time devoted to administration, counseling, meetings, research, and teaching ranges from zero to almost full time. The distribution of a director's time is due in large part to his particular interests and special talents; however, Oetting's figures indicate that a relationship exists between such factors as size of institution, type and level of degree held by the director, size of center, and proportion of time devoted by the director to the range of potential activities.

The director of a center at a small institution may be the only counselor and, therefore, spend a major share of his time in individual counseling; however, as the size of the institution (and center) increases, the proportion of time devoted to counseling by the director decreases. The directors in the largest institutions of my survey carry almost no client load. Only the director of the private university carries close to a full-time client load. An interesting aspect of the myth of the independent practitioner in the independent agency is revealed in the responses of directors when asked about their activities. Directors want to continue to be identified with their professional counseling activities rather than other aspects of their job. Where the director is obviously engaged in little or no counseling, he seems, nevertheless, to need to explain his temporary disengagement or to discuss some case or cases with which he has been working. At one center the director went to great lengths to explain to me that he took a regular turn at exit interviewing and was the primary back-up counselor for the rest of the staff in handling this chore.

Some directors who wish to maintain their professional identity through the activity for which they were specifically trained tend to exaggerate the extent of their counseling load. One director remarked pointedly that faculty and administrators were continually sending him very tough cases. No one on his staff, however, seemed to have the same perception; they indicated that the director had never presented a case in their case review meetings, did not include figures for his clients or contact hours in the counseling center reports, and had rarely been observed greeting or setting an appointment with someone who was obviously a client. This director's efforts to retain his identification as an active professional counselor might be regarded as a bit of harmless self-deception on the part of one person; but Oetting points out that the contact hour mode for directors who say they spend one-quarter of their time in counseling is twenty to twenty-four per week. Oetting attributes this figure to the heavy work load which directors carry; however, on a full-time basis, this figure would multiply out to eighty to ninety-six contact hours per week. From my experience, I feel that these directors' reports are related to the "lies we tell each other" to maintain our myth.

I doubt a director can be effective with his clients if he carries a full-time case load as one-quarter of his activities. His primary concern is his professional identity, which is an integral part of his self-concept. He may need to maintain his own mythology of being the most productive counselor in the center, thus retaining his status with a professional staff which is suspicious of administrative personnel.

To return now to the staffing characteristics of the fourteen centers in my survey, half the centers are staffed predominantly by counseling psychologists, three predominantly by clinical personnel, two by school-oriented guidance personnel, and two staffs are a mixture of the three professional groups. Each center is engaged in individual contacts with students. However, the varied nature of these contacts and the differing personnel reveal some startling contrasts. At one center, in facilities hidden away at the top of several flights of stairs in an ancient gothic building, a small staff of doctoral-level professionals treats the emotional problems of its student patients. The application form for this service is several pages of closely spaced questions covering almost every facet of the potential patient's life. Housed in spacious quarters on the top floor of an immense building at another institution, a very large staff of interns and doctoral-level staff are similarly engaged in therapeutic contacts of indeterminate length with their student clientele. This one, however, requires no application for service and maintains no central records of any type, not even the names and phone numbers of the patients. In a unique split of services, this center supports a branch skills center in a separate building for educational-vocational guidance and reading and study skills assistance. This separate division is staffed primarily by support personnel who have been given on-the-job training for their specialties.

In sharp contrast to these therapeutically oriented organizations is a center staffed principally by guidance-oriented personnel, deeply involved in exit interviews with students leaving the university

21

and in precollege interviews with students having a low probability of succeeding in the institution. Few personal-emotional problems are handled (and then only by one doctoral-level staff member), and records from the registrar's office are required by the counselor prior to any student contact. The counselors also contact students at the request of parents or faculty members and write reports on these conferences for the referring person.

The staff of another center with a nontherapy orientation devotes the bulk of its time and energies to academic advising with lower division students. As in the previous agency, emotional problems are referred to one staff member, the assistant director, who is working toward a doctorate. Most of the individual contacts with students are carried on by graduate students in the counselor education program and two or three interested faculty members picked up part time on the center budget.

A third center in this guidance category is under specific constraint by the president of the university not to engage in psychotherapy. A few cases are carried by the two or three doctoral-level counselors beyond the strict educational-vocational limits implied in the president's restriction, but the staff has little enthusiasm to confront the issue.

About half the centers visited accept responsibility for both educational-vocational guidance and the personal-emotional problems presented by students. However, they differ in methods of handling clients. One group uses an open assignment in which all staff (except, perhaps, practicum trainees) are available to meet with any potential client whatever his problem may be. In the other group, after an intake interview, assignment is made to one of the counselors specializing in a particular problem. Clinical psychologists on the staff work with personal-emotional problems, guidance specialists or vocational counselors are assigned educational-vocational problems. At one of the centers in this latter group, the chief counselor reviews the application form and the record of the intake session and makes the assignment to a counselor. At another of these centers, all staff routinely handle exit interviews; however, a vocational specialist is employed to consult on educational-vocational matters with other staff members. Unexpectedly, this particular center has a heavy clinical orientation (serving as an internship center for psychiatric trainees), and the majority of the referrals come from physicians at the health service.

Two of the largest centers are variations of the captive training center. At both, over 80 per cent of the individual contacts are made by doctoral interns, with the permanent staff acting as supervisors and carrying small demonstration case loads. At one of these centers, advanced or senior interns have supervisory responsibility for first-year trainees. At both, an assistant or associate director coordinates the counseling activities of the staff. Each also employs one assistant director or senior staff member for coordinating research and another for supervising national testing programs. Of the fourteen centers, only these report a lack of clients. Permanent staff identify primarily with the academic departments in which most of them hold rank and devote the major proportion of their time and energies to them. Tenure and promotion come through the departments, with an expected emphasis on research and publications. The interns look forward to positions in counselor education programs at major universities. Few of those interviewed are planning to enter service agency work. Some staff members in each center are engaged in professional activities on campus, but only the directors appear to be heavily involved in activities other than the counseling taking place within the centers. In neither case are the centers engaged in a total program on campus, and the attitudes of the staffs toward the campus can best be described as one of benign neglect. The principal concern of these centers is counselor education, and the environment is almost incidental. Service has a subordinate role to training graduate counselors.

An additional type of service, provided by six of the centers, is the administration of national testing programs (CEEB, GRE, MAT). Four of these employ a staff member full or part time to coordinate research activities. The staffs of two of the centers are heavily involved in exit interviews, while the personnel of two other centers are engaged primarily in academic advising for lower division students. One center has a staff member who coordinates counselor contacts with the residence halls, while, at another, one staff member is responsible for faculty contacts and advisor training. And, in an unusual service activity, one center supports a staff member whose primary role is working with handicapped students and serving on planning and maintenance committees to ensure that plans for new buildings and remodeling of old buildings provide for their needs.

One procedural activity which is common regardless of the kinds of services provided is the instant intake or drop-in. Of the fourteen centers, nine permit immediate access of every potential client to a counselor. Two others work with a modified drop-in, which relies on the receptionist to make an evaluation of a potential client's need to talk with a counselor immediately. The specific procedures for the drop-in vary from center to center, as described by Sinnet and Danskin (1967), but essentially involve the counselor's crossing off blocks of time on their appointment books and making themselves available to talk with a student when he arrives at the center. The interviews may last anywhere from fifteen minutes to an hour, determined by the arrival of another potential client.

Major advantages of instant intake are a sharp reduction in the waiting list and increased efficiency of the professional staff, who can make full use of their scheduled appointment hours. Where students are given appointments for some future date, the no-show rate may be significant. But with instant intake a low rate can be expected as students obviously want help when they have a problem, not a week or two later. The counselor can make contacts with people on campus who can give the students information or assistance, making a regularly scheduled counseling session unnecessary or the first appointment more productive than it would otherwise be. The drop-in (uncluttered by lengthy forms and applications) opens the counseling center doors to many students who would not ordinarily seek professional help. Informal conversations with students on several campuses indicate that a significant number feel that the paper work and scheduling which precede a contact with a counselor are designed to discourage students with small problems from consuming valuable counselor time. The effort to see a counselor is

24

not worth the trouble since the counselors obviously are using these hurdles to protect their time for those with serious problems.

Simple procedural practices can strongly influence the number of students who make use of the center and the types of problems which they present. The more hidden behind application blanks and schedules the staff appears to be, the greater pressure a student with a problem must feel before he approaches the center and waits the required time for his scheduled appointment. Those students who regard their problems as less serious are likely to seek assistance elsewhere and to make the center their last resort. In restricting its clientele primarily to students with critical needs for help, the center can become a largely remedial service.

The outline of the college counseling center which emerges from this decriptive material is not sharp and well defined, important to realize if we are to move from myth to reality. Any organization in which the college counselor works has a low probability of matching the ideals of the training program myth. The fourteen centers are not unique. They confirm information gathered by Magoon in his College Counseling Center Data Bank survey of 1970 (Appendix), which indicates that only a small proportion of college centers are not currently involved in some noncounseling or outreach activities. Moreover, with few exceptions the centers surveyed do not operate as independent agencies free from geographical and administrative connections to other institutional operations. They are becoming increasingly integrated into other parts of the academic and administrative functioning of the college. Have these relationships arisen out of a recognition that the independent agency myth is, for most centers, counterproductive to the health and wellbeing of the organization? The center has little political strength or prestige on the college campus except as it is sponsored and protected by other more powerful units of the institution.

What the counselor-in-training perceives his potential role to be is only an incomplete fragment of the roles he may be asked to perform when he arrives at the service agency. My survey as well as Magoon's Data Bank confirm that counselor is a convenient but only partially descriptive title for a counseling center staff member.

He does counsel with individual clients, but he must also be prepared to move out toward the campus as teacher, consultant, program coordinator, or advisor. Counselor-educator Sorenson (1965) very perceptively pointed out: "It is my belief that the counselor has a unique and important role to play in public education but that he isn't playing it very well. It is my further opinion that unless counselors begin to take cognizance of what is happening in education the important changes in counseling will occur without their advice and consent. Counseling will be forced to change, make no mistake about that, by the same pressures which are affecting other aspects of education."

The warnings and encouragements to change, from those like Sorenson, have gone essentially unheeded by the captive counselor education centers. The model of the counselor has remained essentially that of the passive one-to-one remedial therapist. But service centers (as organizations) have been modifying their activities, as my survey and the Data Bank suggest. They are becoming increasingly involved in problem areas where the counselor's special psychological insight and understanding are applicable.

The survey and Data Bank material, however, show that the transition from the myth of the aloof clinic for unhappy and confused young people to the reality of the assertive center of ferment and activity within the institution is markedly uneven from center to center. The captive centers of training programs have moved the least from the individual contact, remedial model, while some agencies offer such a variety of services that they resemble centers for counseling only to the extent that a fraction of staff time is allocated for talking with students individually.

A revised model for the college counselor is needed to replace that of the clinician-therapist against which he has measured his professional adequacy. The survey and Data Bank information support my contention that the counselor must be more than a competent therapist if he is to contribute fully to the needs of the campus community. The new model must reflect the range of potential activities counselors may be called upon to perform in the service setting without compromising their professional integrity.

26

Professional and
Administrative Issues

THREE

The counseling center is an agency of the college. It exists to provide services for some or all parts of the campus community.
Whether it is primarily a training center or a service agency, its
procedures and objectives will be determined to some extent by the
degrees of freedom allowed it by other parts of the institution. The
staff may, through imaginative application of their skills, increase
the degrees of freedom within which it operates; however, it can
never completely free itself from accountability to and reliance on
other units of the institution.

Limits on the activities in which a center's staff can engage may be set rather directly through the policy statements of higher administrative personnel as in the case of a president's statement that the center is not to offer psychotherapy; withdrawal of a psychology department's faculty or interns; or a set of institutional or state-system guidelines regulating staff conduct and consulting activities. Limits may result from more indirect communications such as information from a faculty member that a significant administrator has been critical of one of the center's programs; the reassignment to another department of a function which has been the responsibility of the center; or lack of cooperation by the head of an administrative unit in a project proposed by the center.

The facts of working life ought to be well understood by counselors, particularly since one of their major tasks is to assist young people to anticipate the demands of the world of work. However, many are distressed when they discover that the center does not have complete freedom to set its own goals and procedures, that political and financial factors are part of the institutional press affecting their activities. Of equal annoyance is the discovery that the center is an organization, not simply the location housing private practitioners. Graduate programs prepare the counselor for his individual counseling, but, unless he has previously been employed, he is often unprepared to cope with the related administrative details. The graduate program gives the counselor a sense of being "professional," but has not clarified what this means beyond his adequacy to handle clients. Many counselors interpret "professional" to mean that they are fully self-directing and that restrictions imposed by the organizational structure are a reflection on their professional status.

The new counselor may arrive on the job expecting to be able to set up his own private practice, not infrequently in the center during working hours. His association with graduate program professors who have established private consulting relationships distorts his perception of acceptable behavior in a service agency. He often seems unconcerned about state laws restricting the practice of psychology to those who have worked in a supervised setting for a year or two subsequent to having received his degree and passed the state qualifying examination. He is even less likely to be aware of state system or university policy requiring him to obtain permission to work for income beyond his base salary, not only for private practice and consulting but also for teaching continuing education courses. One counselor became incensed at the denial of his request to teach an evening course for three successsive terms in a community 120 miles from the college. The college administration rejected the request for more than one term because he would be required to leave his office early during the afternoon of the class and could not return before a late hour at night, thus potentially affecting his job performance the next day. Such restrictions, right or wrong, do exist, and the counselor must be prepared to cope with his feelings about them in other than unproductive, frustrated anger.

Graduate programs have seemed to leave students with a smouldering anti-authority feeling, which may appear on the job as an opposition to structural procedures; as overreactions to the comments of the director perceived as carrying evaluative overtones; or as forgetting the details of administrative or organizational guidelines.

One function of the internship is to help potential counselors make the transition from the academic to the job situation. However, the majority of internship positions for college counseling are located in a center staffed primarily by faculty of the graduate program. The emphasis in this captive center is on training. As with other courses in the department, the performance standards of the student in the particular activity being taught is the only concern of the supervising staff. The student's tasks are defined, and meeting performance requirements is his sole responsibility. The student is protected from such concerns as the ambiguities of campus politics, budget problems, and the pressures of potential client loads. He is also free from the need to justify his productivity when not performing in class, on an exam, or in a supervised interview session.

In contrast, the service agency is interested in the use which the counselor makes of the full time for which he has been employed. When the counselor is not engaged in activities directly related to his client load, he is expected to be working on research, consulting

29

with faculty or students, or otherwise devoting himself to some professional work. He may feel that he is being held more accountable for his activities than are faculty members who appear to come and go as they please, a feeling which might be disputed by the faculty member with several courses to prepare, papers to read, tests to construct and grade, and articles to be published. Salary increases, promotion, and tenure must be justified to administrators who require evidence that the counselor is productively using the time outside his twenty client contact hours per week.

The demands of the training center differ from those of the service agency. The similarity between the two types of center often ends with the fact that both work with clients. Shortly after taking my first position at a service center in a university of ten thousand, I was given responsibility for planning and coordinating the entire new student week program, including the academic advising schedule, the social programming, the room arrangements for all events, and the production of a printed program. Nothing in my graduate school education had prepared me to anticipate this type of work for a counselor. On my second service center job, I was designated as Assistant Head Marshal for commencement with responsibility for considerable clerical detail work before the program and supervision of the line-up, march and seating arrangements for the program. These are examples of unusual activities in which a counselor may become involved. But more important to the effective operation of the center as an organization are the day-to-day administrative and interpersonal details faced by staff which they must work through satisfactorily. The annoyance expressed by counselors when they confront some situations outside the counseling room seems to justify a survey of a few of the most troublesome. They are arbitrarily broken down into several major categories. Obviously, some problem categories overlap and some do not fit easily in any category.

Central to the smooth operation of a counseling center is staff agreement on procedures for handling cases. Although counseling process is a principal focus of counselor education, the context within which counseling is carried out, including clerical details, the impact of service pressures, and agency operating procedures, are typically ignored. It is as if the counselor can take his in-cubicle skills to a service agency and use them without regard to the environment in which he works. Coming from an educational situation in which the emphasis on learning a set of skills gives his needs priority over the need of the center to offer services, the counselor arrives at the service center and is faced by a reversal of these priorities. He discovers that he is expected to carry his share of the load. He will find that rewards do not necessarily accrue to the counselor who fills his schedule with long-term therapy cases. He may even discover that the center has established procedures for assuring client turnover, requiring each counselor to pick up two or three new clients each week or to present any case which reaches ten interviews for staff review. He may find an instant intake system which obligates him to see new clients as they arrive at the center, sometimes without their having completed an application or personal data form. When his schedule is filled, he can experience considerable discomfort in having to choose between adding an intake as an overload or turning over his client to another counselor.

The new counselor discovers that, although case management is no longer determined by a supervisor, he is not a completely free agent in his work. He learns that the center has established minimum standards for number of client contact hours per week, and also that he may have to adapt to procedures developed primarily by a receptionist which affect his case assignments and intrusions on his open time. He may arrive in the morning to find an appointment on his calendar which was not entered when he left the previous afternoon. He may finish an interview to be confronted by an unscheduled client. He may learn that he must justify to the director or coordinator of counseling his intention to reduce his case load or to make significant adjustments in the hours he is available to meet with clients.

When he moves from a counselor education program to a service agency, the counselor must shift his orientation from a very understandable concern with his own welfare to a concern for the effect of his decisions or actions upon the total staff, upon the image of the agency on campus, and upon the students who come to the center for assistance. Little in the counselor's experience as a graduate student encourages him to integrate his activities with those of his peers or to be concerned about institutional needs. Moreover, as a graduate student competing for grades and the positive attention of the faculty, he may have concern about the welfare of his clients, but basically they are important to him as they contribute to his primary goal of successfully completing his degree.

Counseling center records pose another potential problem area for counseling staff. For some new staff, maintenance of records seems to have become so identified with the evaluation procedures of their former supervisors that they resist completing interview write-ups and making clerical notations. The counselor often views requirements for maintaining clerical records as simply administrative harassment. Case notes, rather than being perceived as a means of self-evaluation or a record of development, seem to become identified as an onerous task. Record keeping required on the job is similar to that required in practicum and internships, and therefore tends to evoke student evaluation responses rather than job-oriented responses. The counselor responds as he would have liked to respond in the training situation, by simply ignoring the requirements or engaging in slowdown tactics, misplacing case folders or piling up interview summaries. Few centers seem to have specific guidelines for case note content. I know of only one center which does not maintain some case notes and client records. It seems reasonable, therefore, that counselors would be helped, during their graduate education, to anticipate the record-keeping needs of service agencies and to work through their reactions to clerical details before placing themselves on the job market.

In this same category are problems related to the filing and maintenance of case folders. A number of counselors seem to have little comprehension of the meaning of confidentiality in other terms than those related to questions asked about a client by a dean, parent, or faculty member. While warning his colleagues about the need to protect the counseling relationship against those whom he perceives as snoopers, a counselor will unthinkingly leave a pile of client folders on his desk for anyone to read who happens by, including the janitor and student clerks, or he may take client folders home to type his notes. A counselor who would be offended by the suggestion that he was insensitive to the needs of others on the staff will keep case folders in or on his desk, forcing the receptionist to search, in his absence, for a folder which she may need for some part of her work. From the perspective of the professional these may appear to be minor things; however, from the perspective of clerical staff whose job satisfaction is keyed to their ability to carry out their tasks efficiently and quickly, they can significantly affect morale. Clerical staff do not take kindly to the counselor who asserts his professional independence through actions which increase their work load and unnecessarily complicate their routine.

Other potential sources of professional-clerical staff friction include case assignment and scheduling, work priorities, the willingness of counselors to obtain demographic data from clients and to remind them of unpaid fees, and counselors' removal of materials and supplies from the desks of clerical personnel. I believe that one indication that a staff perceives the counseling center as an organization is a high degree of cooperation between professional and clerical personnel and a mutual respect for each other's work. The counselor who jealously guards his professional prerogatives will quickly be confronted with the fact that clerical staff quite literally control front office operations. The counselors may develop general guidelines for procedures, but details are filled in by the receptionist and secretaries. In making appointments and setting schedules, the counselor has restricted degrees of freedom. The larger the staff, the more difficult it is for the receptionist to make idiosyncratic exceptions to procedures for scheduling appointments. A few common irritants to the receptionist are the counselor's failure to inform or check with her when he makes or cancels an appointment; does not appear for an appointment or leaves the office without informing her; or cancels the same client several times. In each case, the receptionist is generally required to straighten out conflicts, make explanations to annoyed clients, or spend time making unnecessary

33

phone calls. She does not appreciate his leaving her with problems caused by his thoughtlessness.

Work priorities for clerical staff set by the professionals result in negative reactions by the clerical personnel if they are ignored by one or two of the counselors, especially if work is presented regularly as "emergency," thus effectively eliminating the work priority system. Once the professional staff has agreed on priorities within which clerical work is to be handled, the professionals may find it difficult to get their clerical work completed unless everyone follows those priorities except for real emergencies. The counselors would do well to establish a uniform procedure for approving emergency work at the time they set the priorities, because the most serious misunderstandings seem to arise when each counselor sees himself as one of the front office supervisors.

The goal to be aimed for in relations between clerical and professional staff is cooperation, enabling the center to operate smoothly and efficiently with a minimum of self-consciousness regarding rights and privileges. Some counselors unfortunately feel the need to split functions rather sharply and reject any involvement in what they consider strictly clerical matters. When application forms are not complete, they studiously avoid obtaining the necessary information from the client. If the client, for one reason or another, has not paid the counseling or testing fee, they will ignore requests by the receptionist or psychometrist to raise the issue with the client. Theoretically, these matters are the responsibility of clerical staff, but actually it is not always possible for the clerical personnel to handle them easily. For example, where the receptionist is responsible for large numbers of case folders, she is unlikely to remember which clients have not completed their application forms. It is more efficient for the counselor to glance over the form with the client and fill in the missing information. The psychometrist may be reluctant to refuse to administer tests to a student until he has paid his fee. The counselor is in a much better position to discuss the question of fees with the client. Both data and fee collection can be given a much more personal orientation if the professional will assume responsibility for these clerical matters.

Professional and Administrative Issues

A very minor, but potentially explosive issue is the assumption by counselors that the desks of the clerical staff are public property. The typist or secretary who finds her stapler or scotch tape missing, or her desk opened and materials removed is likely to be resentful of the liberties taken with her work space and property. The counselor must not assume that his more prestigeful position gives him rights to invade the work space of clerical staff. Another potential irritant between the professional and the clerical staff is the coffee room. Counselors tend to assume that the making of coffee and the cup clean-up are included in the job descriptions of typists and secretaries. Clerical personnel at several centers have simply refused to serve in this role after counselors began to take the service for granted. If the counselors indicate that they recognize this as an extra chore and show a willingness to do their own clean-up, the coffee room is unlikely to become a battleground. When counselors simply assume that a secretary is also a waitress, they may not only lose their coffee but a measure of good will besides.

Every book about counseling contains a discussion of the in-cubicle deportment of the counselor; I will, therefore, confine my remarks on the relationship between the counselor and client to that outside the counseling room. An agency ought not to have to be concerned about a counselor and client becoming involved in other than their counseling relationship. Nevertheless, I know of instances where a counselor hired clients to help with research projects and, in one of these cases, a client was given a key to the center for after-hours work and was apparently free to roam through the offices. More common is the temptation to become involved with a client socially. In one rather extreme example, a counselor regularly invited clients as guests to his home and became part of the social circle of some of them, receiving and accepting invitations to parties and other social activities. The dangers to the helping relationship in this confusion of professional and social roles by the counselor seem obvious. A counselor who becomes involved socially with clients would seem to be expressing a deficiency in his own psychological structure which needs a counselor's attention. No counselor should be permitted to complete his graduate education without having coped with his own needs as they reveal themselves in the counseling relationship.

As counselors move out of their cubicles, the problems inherent in the counselor-client relationship become more complex. Counselors obviously must become more flexible in their approach to those with whom they are working; meetings with individuals and groups outside the center are not only reasonable, but necessary. However, the counselor must be particularly sensitive to the various interpretations which others may ascribe to these meetings. Taking a socially withdrawn student to the commons for coffee may be appropriate; whereas meeting with a student of the opposite sex in the student's apartment or some secluded room is loaded with the potential for misinterpretation. The counselor's motives may be above reproach, but he must be sensitive to the expectations others have of proper professional conduct, and to the fact that outside his usual professional setting he may have more difficulty in keeping his professional goals and personal needs in perspective. The counselor should confront himself with some difficult questions about his own needs; for instance, if he has an urge to increase the relaxation potential of sessions with a female client by holding his sessions with her someplace outside the center. Young counselors who want to make full use of the more flexible counseling procedures which have come into vogue forget that clients may gain from counseling because counselors do not respond to them as they have come to expect from others. The freer approaches to counseling impose an even greater burden on the counselor to be certain that his own needs do not interfere with a professional counseling relationship.

Good work relationships, including a willingness to share experiences, are essential to an effective counseling center operation. This does not imply that counselors should be personal friends, but it does mean that they should communicate openly with each other on the job. Graduate education does not encourage cooperation with peers, or with authority figures. The pressures for success, as has been mentioned, tend to increase competitiveness, fear of evaluation, and privatism. Some counselors resist presenting their cases in a staff meeting or sharing their on-campus experiences. More than one counselor I have known have refused to tape interviews and rejected every argument about the need for continuing in-service training on the basis that to require them to present cases is a reflection on their professional competence.

Communication with the director has its own potential for problems. One staff of counselors complained at the end of the year that they had not had enough individual contact with the director. In order to ensure more frequent contacts during the following year, the director set aside an hour every week for meeting with each counselor until he discovered, toward the end of the fall term, that two new counselors resented this scheduled appointment as a checking device. In a variation on this suspicion-of-authority syndrome, a senior counselor, who was acting director during a prolonged absence of the director, was subsequently perceived by the other counselors as part of the administration and excluded from many of the informal staff interactions. How widespread this feeling of suspicion and distrust may be among counselors cannot be easily determined, but my informal conversations with directors indicates that the examples are not atypical.

Becoming part of a working staff within a larger organization after several years as a graduate student proves to be a difficult transition for many young counselors. The reaction to this release from student status is often a self-conscious assertion of independence. Since the progress and achievement in graduate school are his own private affair, he needs to be only minimally interested in the total performance of the program. In joining a service agency, his performance becomes the concern of the entire staff, for what he does and how he does it affect the performance of other staff members. Staff meetings in which cases are presented can be a means by which staff become familiar with the strengths and weaknesses, the counseling style, and the philosophical approach of other members of the staff; thus, improving the ability of all staff members to make intra-agency referrals. The fact that centers often recruit with an eye toward diversification of counseling philosophy and counselor strengths makes a counselor's rejection of case presentations rather

37

foolish, for the staff loses the opportunity to learn from its members those things for which, in part, it recruited him.

Similarly, new staff may be reluctant to report what they are doing on other projects on campus. Here again, the reaction to being evaluated gets in the way of overall staff education. The center as an organization can become involved through individual staff members in many campus activities. Some counselors may speak to living groups, others may organize human relations sessions, still others may be members of committees affecting student life. How these counselors are perceived reflects on the total organization and may mean a continuation of potential expansion of some service or activity. On the other hand, a poor reaction can mean a discontinuance of the center's involvement. A counselor, working independently, can therefore commit the rest of the staff to meeting certain expectations or may put an end to a valuable project. Moreover, the total staff need continually to be learning about the procedures that succeed or do not succeed, which groups of students need additional services, what faculty respond favorably or unfavorably to the center and its services, and generally what is happening on the campus. The counseling staff should not be working in a feed-back vacuum. Each member has responsibility for communicating to his colleagues as much relevant information about the campus and his experiences with parts of it as he can. Only in this way can the center become and remain a truly effective organization.

Job assignment can pose a problem for the staff. There are usually necessary tasks within any agency which are more desirable than others, and a new counselor can expect to find himself with a task he might not particularly prefer. If there is no occupational information specialist, he may be asked to receive, evaluate, and file the materials which come to the office. Although he may not see himself as a researcher, he may be asked to help with some ongoing research project. He may be requested to develop some aspect of the in-service training program. In general, counseling staffs attempt to fit new members into areas in which they are most interested, but this is not always possible, and the grace with which the new member accepts a less desirable assignment and his willingness to carry through as well as he can will do much to gain him acceptance by the staff.

The counselor's normal suspicion of authority figures finds a natural target in the psychiatric consultant. The psychiatrist often serves the center in a rather ambiguous role. On some campuses the center may by choice have little contact with whatever psychiatric services are available. Where a psychiatrist does act as a consultant, his role is generally perceived by the staff as the medical "back-up" professional, helpful for his legal coverage, necessary for medication, and an expeditor when diagnosis and hospitalization may be required.

How the psychiatrist perceives his role may be quite a different matter. Trained in the medical tradition of "one man in charge," he may have difficulty accepting a colleague role and can easily convey to counselors through his interactions with them a sense of their lower status. One psychiatrist, hired to consult with professional counselors, spent almost the entire school year encouraging the staff to define his role. The fact that he had a supervisor's role in mind for himself—a role the staff would not accept—made this task impossible and disruptive.

On the other hand, counselors share responsibility for the difficulties they experience in their relationship with the psychiatrist. With an unfortunate lack of discrimination, many counselors respond to all psychiatrists as a threat and resist any meaningful involvement with them. This may take the form of passive aggression expressed as a reluctance to discuss cases or engage in dialogue with the psychiatrist. Conversely, it may take the form of the counselor's falling into the student role and allowing the psychiatrist to teach him about case management. In either situation, the potential richness of positive interactions between professionals with different training is lost. It would seem that in this relationship, too, the counselors have not been prepared to work as equal team members with those from other disciplines. In counselor education, the psychiatrist has too often been the instructor, and neither the counselor nor the psychiatrist is oriented to the give-and-take of colleagues.

The most serious relationship problems of the professional

counselor in a service agency result from the fact that his position forces him to straddle organizational fences within the institution. He is too much a part of the student personnel administrative structure to be fully accepted by faculty as academic personnel and oriented too much toward academic values to be fully accepted by the administrators as student personnel professionals. His deeper involvement in student services than classroom teaching or research lowers his status in the eyes of faculty, while his giving higher priority to student service than to institutional procedures makes him suspect among personnel people. His tenuous part-time connections with teaching departments give him little direct influence in the academic community. On the other hand, his confidential relationships with students and his tendency to sympathize with students in their quarrels with the institution make him appear to be a poor team member in student personnel. This list could easily be extended.

Despite the stereotype of the counselor as an agent of adjustment, the great majority of counselors in my experience have had one thing in common—a devotion to change. They are continually participating in the process of helping individuals and groups to modify perception or behavior, not to fit into the environment more easily but rather to be able to act on the environment as freer and more independent human beings. They are sensitive to the contradictions and inequities within the institution and they tend to ally themselves with students and their concerns. These are commendable qualities in the abstract. They are not, however, the characteristics of those who wield direct power in the institution, nor are they characteristics which bring ready acceptance from either faculty or administrators.

Faculty are willing to tolerate a counseling center as long as it seems to relieve them of troublesome student contacts and facilitates the movement of marginal students out of the department. However, I know of several instances when academically superior students were discouraged from going to the center by faculty concerned that these good students might decide to change majors while talking to a counselor. In another instance, faculty of a department became annoyed with several counselors who assisted students in the department arrange a faculty-student confrontation. Probably every director has received phone calls from incensed faculty members complaining that, after talking with a counselor, some student has decided to take an action which the faculty member had previously tried to convince the student not to take. Communication with faculty must be a continuing process, both by the agency and by individual counselors. The activities of the center are, by and large, of very low priority interest to all but a comparatively few faculty. For some, such special services as counseling are little more than coddling students and they look on the center with contempt. For others who may themselves have had a poor experience with a counselor or therapist or know someone who has, all counselors are at best inept and should be avoided. No amount of factual information in printed material, such as a faculty newsletter, newspaper articles, or brochures, will convey to the majority of the faculty what the center can do.

Although printed material has some value, personal contacts by counseling staff with faculty, both individually and in groups, has a much better chance of having a positive impact, assuming that the counselors do not convey a smugness or arrogance about their professional activities. The best communication with faculty is the completion of a good job for a sympathetic faculty member. Word moves quickly across a college campus. If the center helps one faculty member with a problem, it will soon have other requests for the same service. Conversely, if one counselor engages in a questionable activity or fails to carry through on a request, the entire staff must live with the consequences. Perhaps because in many institutions the center is perceived as part of the student personnel structure, it is always somewhat suspect to the academics and particularly vulnerable when its staff is felt to be either too visible or too unreliable in serving the needs of the campus community.

With the common and logical attachment of the counseling center to student personnel services for budgeting and administrative purposes, counselors find themselves in an uneasy alliance with other personnel staff. Philosophically and temperamentally, professional counselors are not administrators. On the other hand, despite

41

Williamson's contention, administrators are not counselors (1961). It is true, of course, that some excellent deans have come from the ranks of the professional counselors (usually after they have spent some time directing a center), and that some deans have been involved in warm and sensitive relationships with students. But the two professional groups march to different drummers.

The dean should be concerned about the welfare of students as a total group, but his first responsibility must always be to the central administration of the institution. The students know this. Not one of the students in a graduate course for student personnel workers which I have taught for several years has denied it, and this is the issue, in fact, which has most seriously put them in conflict with their ideals.

The counselor, on the other hand, by training and by the ethical codes of his profession, is committed first to the clients with whom he is working. Only in the case of serious threat to others or to the client himself is the counselor to deviate from his responsibility to maintain his client's confidences. The counselor is frequently the quiet advocate in the student's battles with parts of his environment. As the counselor moves into the community, his role is no less the assistance of people to cope with—and sometimes to oppose—the status quo. This can bring him into disagreement with others in student personnel and throw into sharp relief the basic differences in orientation. To paraphrase one counselor: "The dean looks after the welfare of a student by explaining the statistical probabilities to him. My job is to help the student defeat the statistics if he feels that is in his own best interest."

Although this difference in orientation is played down by writers in student personnel, nevertheless, counselors and deans sense the difference. The power and authority is generally in the hands of the deans; so open conflict is rare. By and large, the only weapon the counselor has (except for personal ties to others on campus who may have power) is his resignation; but I know of just one staff which, as a group, resigned over a dispute with a dean of students. More commonly, the tension is expressed through a form of passive resistance by the counselors and an insistence on bureaucratic compliance with rules and regulations and detailed reports on the part of the dean. This is an effective ploy because it reminds the counselor that he is not faculty. Having no administrative authority or responsibility, the counselor feels keenly his vulnerability and his alienation from the academic community. His being on the fringe of the system probably increases the counselor's sensitivity to environmental pressures and his identification with the students with whom he works, but his alienation has the parallel effect of heightening his feelings of insecurity in the work situation. The point is simply that the student personnel administrator is part of the system—the administrative team—while the counselor, with nothing to administer, and at best only a tenuous connection to an academic department, is a marginal man in both power systems and unlikely to be a loyal team member in either.

The counselor does not make a good politician. Those qualities which characterize the effective counselor—openness, a desire to encourage the optimum use of individual talents in others, and an opposition to arbitrary or imposed authority—unfit him to manipulate people or events to achieve some personal or organizational goal. To those familiar with the use of power, he appears naive in his direct use of confrontation or resistance. However, even if he has developed a political sense, a member of the counseling staff is in an extremely vulnerable position from which to become a political force on campus. This is not the place to discuss the meaning or sources of campus power, but it should be pointed out that, with few exceptions, power resides in departments and schools in rough approximation to their status in that particular academic community. An individual, unless he has charisma or connections to other sources of influence, draws on that ascribed power in proportion to his status within his academic unit. Student personnel, except in very limited areas, have relatively little authority in the college. Since the counseling center is marginal to both academic and student personnel structures, what power or influence any one person in the center may have would be drawn from an extremely small organizational supply. In a few instances through longevity or personal contacts with powerful faculty or both, a member of the center may have access to one or two of the smaller handles of political influence. The amount of power the center derives from student personnel is usually zero. In fact, for the center staff to make effective contributions to the academic community and to the student body, they must frequently disclaim their connections with the student personnel structure.

Unfortunately for the effectiveness of the total student personnel program, deans of students may feel threatened if members of the center become too closely identified with academic departments. If the dean of students senses that he is suspect by faculty and is viewed as having a low status position in the campus community, a counselor who appears to identify with the academic community through teaching or research or both runs the danger of stirring up the resentments of the person on whose team he is supposed to be playing. One young counselor was shaken when he discovered that his efforts to develop contacts within the psychology department were an annoyance to the dean of students, who confronted him with implications of disloyalty and insisted that he make a clear choice between his student personnel and academic ties. The fact that the counselor was currently neither faculty nor administrator—and recognized the fact for the first time—made the confrontation even more distressing. In another case, an experienced counselor found himself repeatedly faced by his dean with the dilemma of what he was or should be. The counselor had developed a reputation for his writing and had received excellent evaluations on his part-time teaching by his students. Despite the fact that the counselor enjoyed the combination of activities, the dean was not at all subtle in urging him to move out of counseling and devote himself full time to academic work. The game which the counselor must play to maintain acceptability to both the academic community and the student personnel group, while retaining his professional self-respect, is a difficult one. The loss of many counselors to full-time teaching positions or to administrative positions seems to confirm that some find the pressures to commit themselves totally to one or the other are simply too great to withstand.

This chapter certainly does not exhaust the range of difficul-

44

Professional and Administrative Issues

ties faced by members of a counseling service agency. Hopefully, these selections will bring to the attention of potential college counselors and to the faculty of counselor education programs areas of concern for the professional counselor. The preparation of counselors should include some consideration of these problems and a thorough airing of attitudes toward them so that the new staff member will be able to anticipate the difficulties he is most likely to confront on the job. Too many counselors, experiencing their first work situation, feel that these or other problems are unique to the center in which they have chosen to work. Only after moving once or twice to avoid these difficulties does he become aware that variations on familiar themes appear in each center. He discovers that, unless he gives up counseling service work altogether, he must learn how best to cope because he cannot escape them.

New Roles for

Counselors

FOUR

It is unexpected to some that the annual presentation at the American Personnel and Guidance Association convention of innovative procedures, in which counseling centers have engaged through the previous year, are primarily devoted to noncounseling activities. The professional counselors' participation in in-service training programs for advisors, consultation with faculty and student groups, study skills programs, human relations groups, and a variety of other functions relates only tangentially to the emphasis in counselor education (Appendix).

The innovations go beyond an adaptation of counseling

techniques to new publics or different situations. They represent a fundamental change in job orientation. The classical counselor has been defined by writers and counselor educators as a receptive helper. Time not devoted to individual counseling was to be spent conducting research, preferably on counseling effectiveness or counseling process. The counseling room was the domain, often the limit, of his campus experience. The student must seek him out, for only the self-motivated client could profit from the service he could offer. Thus, the effort required of the potential client to find him, fill out the application form, endure the waiting list, and face the uncertainties of an unknown experience with a stranger became the test of adequate motivation to qualify for the service of a professional counselor.

This self-contained process has reduced the potential for challenge by the student consumers to the work of professional counselors on the campus. The onus for seeking assistance or continuing in counseling has been placed squarely on the shoulders of the student clientele. Typically, counselors have carefully defined the limits of their responsibility to a client, making clear to him at the end of a session that the scheduling of another appointment was his decision. "No shows" have been attributed to the client's lack of motivation to make sufficient personal investment in the process. The client who hesitated in responding to the usual nonspecific invitation to return when he felt the need to talk to someone has been similarly dismissed as acting out his resistance to upsetting his status quo. Counselors have too frequently concealed their ineffectiveness in working with a client or their unwillingness to share responsibility with the client for the progress of counseling behind an assumption of low motivation or client resistance.

The emerging approach to counselor responsibility is distressing to traditionalists, for it requires the professional counselor to move out of his cubicle into the campus community and conduct some of his activities under public scrutiny. It compels the counselor to be sensitive to forces in the institutional environment which are contributing to student distress, but, beyond observation, to evaluate the effect of these forces on students and to take appropriate action.

47

Secondly, this new approach requires the counselor to seek out new locales and novel techniques for service—no longer simply a passive listener, but rather an active participant in the campus community. Thirdly, this approach requires that the counselor abandon his reliance on remedial services and adopt an active preventative and developmental strategy for his functions.

Students have begun to insist on meaningful human contacts (Sanford, 1967). They have been critical of the lack of congruence between academic requirements and the life for which they see themselves being prepared. They have condemned the growing depersonalization within our institutions and pointed out that their intellectual performance is dependent on concern for their personal-emotional development. Moreover, students from ethnic minorities have emphasized the inability of college personnel to understand and accept their unique needs and life styles. By remaining silent and uninvolved, the counseling center has appeared to be uninterested in general student concerns and, therefore, a part of the adult resistance to change. As an "island of calm" for a relatively few students motivated to play the counseling game by rules devised by the professional counseling staff, the center's impact on campus has been minimal. Counseling is a highly verbalized invention designed to cope most effectively with the problem-solving need of a motivated middle-class clientele willing to postpone their gratifications, and therefore has value to a decreasing proportion of an increasingly heterogeneous student population. Innovation has been overdue in restructuring the services of college counseling center staff to improve their versatility and make their presence on campus significant to greater numbers of students. Adding staff to increase traditional services is not the solution to the problem confronting college counseling centers.

Ironically, the debate over appropriate new roles for counselors is academic because the roles of professional counselors are already undergoing modification on numerous campuses. Of sixty counseling centers on major college campuses which I surveyed in 1968, the director of only one indicated that counseling was the sole activity engaged in by his staff. Individual counseling tends to remain a primary focus of professional staff, but other activities—about which few counselors-in-training are informed and fewer still receive any preparation—are being given increasing emphasis. Some of these activities can hardly be considered innovations; however, they do indicate a changing attitude toward the service of professional counselors from customary procedures restricted to contact with one person at a time to a variety of procedures having an impact on groups of students or affecting the entire campus community; from a passive service role to a more aggressive search for various methods of serving the campus community in meaningful ways.

The shift from a sole reliance on counseling with individuals to more diversified services is not motivated merely by theoretical or idealistic considerations. Virtually every counseling center faces the problem of inadequate staff allocation to offer individual counseling to all students who may need help. If a norm of twenty-five contact hours per week is used as a base for full-time counseling load, and three contacts is used as an average number of contacts per client, then each full-time staff member would be expected to counsel with approximately 250 clients per school year and invest 750 to 800 contact hours in his individual counseling. Thus, four full-time counselors would be required to service each thousand student clients. A college of ten thousand would require six full-time counselors to meet the individual counseling needs of 15 per cent of its students or eight full-time counselors to meet the counseling needs of 20 per cent of its student body.

These hypothetical figures are optimistic because twenty contact hours per week is the more usual standard for a full-time counselor. Moreover, student use of counseling services tends to be low during examination weeks, the first week or two of each term, and periods which present conflicts or personal inconvenience to students, thus reducing the number of potential counseling contact hours actually available. Of sixty centers in major colleges and universities responding to another of my surveys during 1970, only a few had a ratio of one full-time professional counselor for each thousand students. The majority had ratios of one counselor for each four or five thousand students. Thus, the possibility of contact with a maximum of only 4 to 6 per cent of the student body in individual counseling is the ultimate potential of some college counseling centers. The conclusion seems obvious. In the centers of our major state colleges and universities, not more than 4 to 15 per cent of the student body could hope for individual counseling from professional staff, even if the highest potential contact hour figures are used.

More typically than most college counselors like to admit, one-quarter to one-third of their contacts with students are single enriched advice or referral sessions. While these contacts may be valuable, if only as an entree to the center for students who may subsequently need additional assistance, their purpose might more efficiently be accomplished through other procedures or by other members of the campus community or both.

These one-contact cases pose problems for the professional counselor beyond the fact that they consume time potentially reserved for more serious problems. First, counselors in their training receive little encouragement to evaluate quickly and make prompt concise decisions about the appropriate disposition of a case. The emphasis on counseling procedures makes them reluctant to commit themselves on a situational decision or to supply information within the first contact. Professional counselors are inclined to suspect some more complicated problem. Second, the counselor, when asked for simple information or assistance in finding an appropriate person who can help, feels frustrated because his counseling skills have not been needed. Many counselors have difficulty in collecting the information necessary to evaluate a presented problem quickly, preferring to use techniques reinforced in their graduate education: passive listening and depth probing. The presented problem may receive little attention while the counselor searches for the real reason the client came to the center, and the session ends with some superficial advice or a poorly thought-through referral. Traditional counselors also show little inclination to prepare themselves to work as part of an institutional mental health network by spending the time necessary to identify and meet with potential referral sources on campus, feeling their time better spent in talking with additional clients. This results in students without problems requiring professional counseling being sent off to unsympathetic faculty or inappropriate offices.

The assumption by counselors of novel service roles is not simply a matter of permitting them direct contact with more students in a given amount of time, although the institution of some new procedures may have this effect. The more fundamental questions being raised by counseling staffs are whether the traditional in-cubicle role makes optimum use of their resources, and whether some student needs might not be better met by other techniques. For instance, if groups are begun primarily to make efficient use of staff time, the counselors may be disappointed. Interview time is required for selecting appropriate group members. Scheduling often requires repeated phone calls. The sheer frustration of finding a common time period for eight or ten students to meet hardly seems worth the effort if time saving is the only criterion by which the value of a group is judged. However, evaluated from the perspective of the types of problems presented by prospective clients, a group may be a more appropriate technique for a counselor to use in working with those particular students than meeting with each individually. For students having difficulty with interpersonal relationships, or for those whose value structure is being shaken by their college experience, the individual interview method may be the least effective procedure available to the counselor. Learning new ways of interacting with people requires practice and the development of a sensitivity to one's impact on others. What better way of learning these functions than to practice in a group of peers with a trained leader available for protection and encouragement? What better way for a student to work through his value conflicts than with peers who are confronting a similar problem?

Any activity in which the professional counselor engages (including individual counseling) must be evaluated on the basis of mental health criteria first. Once having established that certain goals are desirable, the counselor must decide on the most effective

51

method for reaching those goals. He can no longer assume that his contribution to improved mental health on the campus ends with offering individual counseling.

In addition to its recognition that some types of student problems are more effectively handled by methods other than individual counseling, the counseling staff is confronted with problems common to groups of students which are so pervasive that the counselors have no choice but to work outside the center within the campus community if they are to have any significant part in their solution. For example, the transition from high school to college can be a difficult period for the student. Figures on freshman attrition in our public colleges indicate that one-third to one-half of an entering class leave, are dropped, or do not return after the summer break. Not all of those academic casualties are willing participants in the final decision not to continue. Marriage among women and financial difficulties among the men are common reasons given for leaving college; however, these causes are generally collected in a brief, required exit interview or on a checkout form after the decision has been made. These reasons are socially acceptable both to the student and to the college. The student is saved the embarrassment of having to examine his possible inability to cope with the academic or social demands of the college experience. College personnel are relieved of the necessity of questioning the freshman program and expending efforts to improve the high school-college transition. With the faculty taking the position that those who leave or are dropped have only themselves to blame, the academic community has shown little concern for the loss of human potential.

The counseling staff, however, cannot ignore the potential psychological dislocation of young people who, having set one goal, unexpectedly change their plans or have their plans changed for them. Professional counselors, employed to assist students with their decision making, must assume some responsibility for ensuring that the discontinuities in the lives of the students inherent in the transition from high school to college are not a major human loss; also they must assist students to cope with problems common to the freshman experience which may result in many who are intellectually capable leaving college. This requires that the counseling staff initiate programs which deal with the concerns of students as they evolve during the freshman year. Many questions, ranging from simple procedural inquiries to more complex psychological confusions, are now presented to the staff as individual counseling cases by a relatively small proportion of each freshman class. The individual counseling with new students is often a repetitive procedure, wasteful of counselor time and of dubious general value. What is needed is a more imaginative programming in which "freshman woes" can be dealt with where the students are located and by methods which permit counselor contacts with the majority of the potential clientele. This may mean that the counselor becomes an integral part of an ongoing orientation program, or it may require the center staff to offer special services to groups of freshman students before they encounter problems which result in leaving school.

It seems quite reasonable that help with vocational decision making could be made more widely available through novel approaches to the process. Group techniques in which students work on their concerns and confusions with peers might actually make the process more meaningful. If vocational counseling is to help students learn how to go about making decisions as well as assisting them to make immediate decisions, it follows that the sharing of ideas with others in a similar predicament should be a richer experience than the master-pupil tutorial system of individual counseling. Individual contacts could be made available to those who prefer to talk personally with a counselor or for those who wish to explore personal concerns at greater depth than is possible through vocational group techniques. For the majority of vocational decision-making cases, however, the one-to-one contact is a repetitive and inefficient educational instrument.

The counselor as a facilitator of student self-evaluation and decision making often finds himself assisting the student to resist the pressures generated by the policies and rules established by institutional administrative units. Professional counselors recognize that their effectiveness with individual students in counseling is related to their disassociation from the power structure of the institution.

53

New Myths and Old Realities

The logical assumption has been that students would be more open in discussing their problems with someone who was not identified with any of the judicial and administrative units of the institution. In one sense this is true. The student who fears some disciplinary action is likely to be able to examine his situation more candidly with a person who cannot use self-revealed information against him. A student will be more open about himself if he knows that what he reveals will not be used in making decisions about him.

However, the professional counselor, by his total disengagement from the institutional decision-making structure, may be concentrating his energies under a protective image of neutrality to a small number of students, while neglecting opportunities to improve institutional procedures beneficial to large groups of students. Students select their friends from those people who are willing to commit themselves openly on significant issues. The counselor's neutrality can have a negative effect on the students' opinions of him. By his silence on institutional procedures affecting students, the counselor may be viewed by his prospective clientele as accepting those procedures. This may be much more damaging to the image he wishes to convey to students than for them to know that he is working actively to bring about changes for their benefit.

Following, are a few examples of active involvement of counselors on the campus and their results. After the appointment of one of the counseling staff to the academic deficiencies committee at my institution, the counseling center case load increased through referrals from that committee. One of the counselor's objectives as a member of the committee was to increase the sensitivity of the faculty members to factors other than grade point level in their decisions about students in academic difficulty. The result was a humanizing and individualizing of the committee's approach to students in academic difficulty. Providing assistance to a student became as important as questions of suspension or probation. Subsequently the committee began its first research into the characteristics of students in academic difficulty and the effect of deferring suspension for some students who were academically subject to suspension.

In another case, a counselor, as a member of the New Student Program Committee, was able to encourage the Committee toward a recommendation to the appropriate administration offices for a complete revamping of the orientation program for new students, including increased time for individual academic advising and open time for those needing educational-vocational planning contacts with the professional counselors. In a third case, a counselor serving as a member of the Faculty Senate persuaded his faculty colleagues to postpone passage of a proposal to admit disadvantaged students below the stated admissions standards until the proposal was amended to include provisions for special counseling and remedial programming for those students. And finally, as a consultant to the Academic Requirements Committee, a counselor was able to encourage the members of the Committee to accept other than medical reasons for students dropping courses after the "no penalty" drop date. The result was that the committee, for the first time, began to consider requests on the basis of psychological reasons if these were affirmed by a staff member of the counseling center or the university psychiatrist.

The list could be expanded at some length. The professional counselor, therefore, need not remain passive but can involve himself in the campus community for the general welfare of students. This is not social engineering. The purpose of the counselor's involvement is not the manipulation of people to improve their efficiency or increase their output for the benefit of the organization, but rather to modify the procedures of the institution to conserve human resources and humanize the institution's impact on students. These goals are compatible with those for individual counseling. The focus of the counselor's attention, however, has shifted from the individual student's efforts to cope with his environment to factors in the institution which restrict or impede numbers of students from making optimum use of their potentials or a successful transition from one set of circumstances to another. The traditional counselor may be perceived by students as an adjunct of the establishment and his work as a manipulative device to engineer consent to the prevailing standards unless he is willing to assist in modifying institutional procedures for the benefit of students.

The value of one-to-one counseling by professional counselors is currently being questioned by institutional administrators. In the competition for available funds, it is increasingly classified as a luxury item because its cost per student contact is high. For some students, counseling can be a valuable process for clarifying direction or self-identity. However, many students are hurt psychologically by bureaucratic procedures which were designed to regulate small homogeneous student bodies but have become increasingly depersonalized. Other students feel powerless and manipulated when the institution shifts its priorities for allocating resources or changes the standards for programs and neglects to anticipate the impact on the students. The application of psychological Band-Aids to individual students through counseling can be a valuable service for those students, but it is a futile endeavor unless it is coupled with attempts to reduce the incidence of the psychological casualties. It is particularly frustrating when the counselor knows that the sources of some of the casualties are built into institutional procedures which could be modified.

The term counseling center has an unfortunate restricting connotation, implying that the services of the staff should be centralized within the confines of however many rooms the center has been allocated. Obviously, certain functions—such as testing, research and record keeping—are more efficiently carried out within a centralized location, but the centralization of professional personnel can result in the staff assuming a "fixed-service" mentality. Activities outside the center are perceived as "extra" rather than as an integral part of the job. This fixed-service concept is reinforced by the requirements of the typical counseling center annual report in which the value of the counseling personnel is justified primarily by a tally of clients and counseling contact hours. Thus tied to quantitative measures of traditional service, the director and staff lose their flexibility for considering potential contributions to students outside the individual counseling framework.

As members of a profession oriented toward assisting people

to achieve the maximum development of potentials and greater tolerance for ambiguity, counselors have in general shown remarkable restraint in making full use of their own potentials and an unfortunate rigidity in conceptualizing new or creative roles for themselves in the college community. Students need more than the treatment services of the traditional psychological clinic. They also need more than the usual student personnel services, for even the most sympathetic administrators of these services are locked in formal administrative lines of responsibility. As a consequence, the student personnel administrator does a much better job explaining institutional policies to students than he does interpreting student concerns to other administrators. Moreover, when student concerns touch on academic and faculty matters, student personnel administrators are reluctant to become involved outside their assigned lines of administrative responsibility. The housing director, for instance, is not likely to raise questions about poor grading practices or inadequate advising procedures. The ambiguous position of the counseling staff in the campus community permits them greater freedom to become involved with issues related to students across various administrative lines than is possible for student personnel administrators who are identified by faculty and students with the rules and standards of the institutional establishment.

A counseling center staff must alter its services as the institution changes in size, character and student population. It must adapt its techniques and procedures to the needs of an increasingly diverse student population which is turning more frequently for assistance to other resources than those formal services made available by the institution. For some types of problems students have begun to rely on their peers and others in and around the campus community for help. Under these conditions, the counseling staff is missing an opportunity to use its skills if it does not offer its professional resources to these peer and lay helpers for improving work with students. The counseling by the professional staff obviously cannot be abandoned for it does have value for students with certain types of problems, but the staff cannot ignore its responsibilities to the general welfare of students. It needs to be continually evaluating

57

its role on campus in relation to the conservation and implementation of human potentials within the total student body. This will undoubtedly necessitate a reordering of time and energy priorities.

The traditional counselor role is based on a relationship model. The counselor's developing rapport with the client has been assumed to be critical for successful counseling. If an individual client does not feel confident in the person to whom he goes for counseling, a relationship does not develop and counseling for that client is a failure. If a group of potential clients do not have confidence in the ability of the professional staff of a counseling center to handle some particular problem, they will not use the counselors for assistance and will look to other sources of help. This has been true for several problems which have concerned segments of the student population over the past few years: the draft, abortion, and drugs.

Each of these student crisis situations seems to have one thing in common. They contain anti-institutional or antisocietal components. They are perceived by students as uniquely youth problems only vaguely understood, and most probably rejected, by the majority of adults with official roles in the institution. The result has been that the students have for the most part bypassed the formal counseling services of the institution and created their own crash pads, clinics, hot lines and referral resources. In some cases, individual counselors have, by their personal life styles and personality, retained contact with the student culture and become incorporated into the student self-help network, but it seems that counseling centers as total service operations have been notable failures in meeting these critical needs of students. The pregnant girl, the potential draft resister and the student hooked on drugs are unlikely to walk into a counseling center to ask for help from any counselor who may be available, except as a last resort. Mental health clinic psychologists who are part of the student health service may have greater contact with these student crises through referrals from physicians who become unwilling participants in the bad trips and sexual mistakes of students. The counseling center as an agency is not generally included as a potential resource service where these disruptions in the lives of college-age students are concerned.

That this campus phenomenon is occurring should emphasize for professional counseling staff that they have been catering to a selective group of students with a limited range of problems. Their ability to do a successful job with those students who have come to them has obscured the fact that students with different psychological difficulties may not have been using their services. These other students, like the blacks in their ghettos and the Indians on their reservations, could be overlooked as long as they did not become noisy and call attention to themselves. The surfacing of draft, abortion and drug problems has highlighted for professional counselors a situation which has probably existed since the first counseling center was established. No center is perceived by all students as a place to take all problems for solution. Every center is highly selective in the clientele who will seek out its services, and unless the counselors reverse the process and seek out the problem areas which might use their attention, they will be unaware of the many student needs they are neglecting.

An example of this "hidden need" effect was pointed out to our local counseling center staff a few years ago when one counselor decided to contact the head resident of one of our residence halls and to offer to meet with those students in the hall who had received "down slips" after the mid-term grading period. The head resident agreed to publicize the meeting for an evening during the following week. A majority of the students who appeared were recluses. They had few friends, never talked to their instructors, left their rooms only for meals and classes, and generally knew nothing about the campus and its resources. This was a group of students who would never have come to the counseling center for help; they did not even know that it existed.

The center has potential clientele on campus about which it is doing very little. The emergence of draft, abortion and drug problems confronts the staff with this fact in a way which it cannot rationalize away. However, these particular problems present a special difficulty for professional counselors in that the students affected have more confidence in their peers and others whom they specially select to help them than they do in professional counselors. Therefore, if the professional counselors are to be of assistance, they must work with and through those in whom the students have placed their confidence. The entire staff cannot expect to have the skills for handling each of these unique crises. Each requires specialized knowledge and techniques. Each requires current information about specific legal and treatment resources. The professional counselors do, however, understand counseling processes which can be valuable to those who work directly with the students in trouble. It is in the training of the selected students, faculty and other campus personnel where professional counselors can make their most significant contribution to the campus community.

Moreover, even if the professional counselors were equipped to handle the direct services, they would be unable to do an adequate job. The crisis nature of many of these problems, particularly those related to drugs, necessitates a twenty-four-hour per day crash pad or hotline service. From a strictly pragmatic standpoint, the limited number of professional counselors simply do not have the physical capacity to cover this type of service personally. Thus, the professional counselors are forced to develop a different service role if they wish to be involved effectively in these student difficulties.

The shift from a direct counseling role to that of consultant to lay counselors is not simple. Gordon (1965) has indicated in his excellent article on the training of subprofessionals that the traditional counselor resists breaking down his job into components which are useful and meaningful to nonprofessionals and working in a supervisor-subordinate relationship with trainees. As he points out, most counselor training is carried out as a modeling experience. However, the training needs of counselors working at a drug crash pad or with a distraught pregnant coed may be quite different than those of a professional counselor who attempts to develop an ongoing relationship with his client. The professional counselor has no choice but to learn how to make his skills and knowledge available to others in the campus community already working with these special problems. To ignore the needs of large numbers of

60

students would be to admit that the services of professional counselors are, indeed, of a very limited value to the general student population.

Another result of the increasing diversity of the student population is that the counseling center staff is being confronted with a growing number of marriage problems as the proportion of married students increases. These problems require the counselor to assume yet another role for, although the techniques of counseling are used, it is a type of counselor-client interaction which places him in an unfamiliar position. He must learn to respond in appropriate ways to two people engaged in a mutual difficulty. If he chooses to use a group approach with several couples, he has a still more complicated task than he has faced in his counselor education. He must learn different interaction techniques and he will quickly recognize that the basic model of his counselor education program is inadequate to this new role.

Again, the counseling staff is being asked for a service with which most of its members are unfamiliar and very few are fully prepared to offer, but a task which it must undertake if it is to serve adequately an important part of the student population. Difficulty in his marriage relationship can result in a student's becoming an academic casualty as decisively as his having made a poor educational choice as an entering freshman. Since a higher proportion of upperclassmen and graduates are married than freshmen and sophomores, they are the students most likely to require marriage counseling. Since they have already proved themselves capable of succeeding academically, meeting their need for this service may, in fact, yield a higher return to the institution on the investment of professional staff time than offering increased educational guidance to struggling freshmen. Certainly the institution should protect its investment in these students, and the counseling center, therefore, has considerable justification in helping students who have encountered difficulties in their marriage which can affect their academic progress.

Summarily, the traditional counseling role is inadequate to meet the needs of the contemporary student population. With growing numbers of students and an increasing heterogeneity of student population, the center staff will serve a smaller proportion of students needing assistance unless it develops new and creative methods of offering its services.

One major requirement for the counseling staff is that it move out of the counseling center cubicle and become more active as agents of change on campus. The staff must also develop methods of working with others who can offer direct services more effectively —particularly in problem areas such as the draft, abortion and drugs, where students are turning to their peers and others in whom they have more confidence and direct access than they do to the professional counseling staff. The professional counselors must begin to learn those things necessary for training the direct contact personnel to do a better counseling job.

With increasing numbers of students marrying while in college, professional counselors must also learn those special skills which they will need to work effectively with couples. Since upperclassmen and graduate students are more likely to be married, services for couples would seem to be a justifiable activity for the center because these students have already proved themselves academically and represent a considerable investment of time and money by the institution.

Professional
Standards in
Counselor Training

FIVE

The college counseling center is in a paradoxical position—the greater its investment in the counseling of individuals, the less general impact it has on the solution of student problems. Able to serve no more than 5 to 15 per cent of the student body in individual counseling, it is restricted to remedial functions with a fraction of those distressed students who do not find adequate help elsewhere.

The case load is not randomly selected from those students with problems. Any particular student's learning about the center through news releases and brochures obviously involves a number of chance factors. Referrals from faculty are limited to those relatively few who are sympathetic to professional counseling and feel comfortable in encouraging a student to seek professional help. A significant number of students simply resist presenting any problem to a professional "shrink" and, therefore, do not use the center's services. On this last point, evidence from several unpublished center surveys indicates that few students select the counseling center as a primary source of assistance with their problems; the overwhelming majority indicate that they would go first to parents, friends, faculty and others whom they know personally.

Moreover, each center has a campus image: where there is no separate psychiatric or clinical service in the institution, the image may be that of a psychological clinic for emotionally disturbed students; in other institutions, it may be seen as little more than a vocational testing bureau. Whatever the image, some students will not seek help or accept referral because they do not perceive their problems as appropriate for the staff of the center to handle. The results of local center surveys confirm that a center's image tends to be very specific and that an individual student is likely to perceive it primarily as of value for one type of problem. And finally, staffing of the majority of centers is minimal (frequently no more than one counselor for each three or four thousand students). The total case hour capacity would permit only a small fraction of the student body to be seen in individual counseling even under optimum conditions.

One conclusion from the above facts is that the center serves a select group of students in individual counseling. The selection is based on factors only marginally related to general student needs. It occurs through default rather than by a decision of the staff to meet the highest priority needs of the student body. Most counselors would have difficulty answering the question: why do you service this 5 to 15 per cent of the student body rather than some equally needy group? "Because they happen to be the ones who find us.

Because they have been willing to accept a referral from someone who understands our services. Or, because they have problems which fit the skills of our staff" seem inadequate answers when more than half of any college group have problems which could probably benefit from some sort of counseling.

On the other hand, the presence of a counseling center on campus (no matter how poorly staffed) may have the effect of increasing the depersonalization of contacts between students and faculty. A busy faculty member, when faced with a student who wants to work through some personal feelings or vocational plans, can rid himself of the responsibility for that student by encouraging him to take his problems to the center. "The purchase of friendship" syndrome can replace the informal contacts of adult and young person. If a student refuses to accept a referral to a professional, it may mean that the student is left with his problem plus confirmation of his suspicion that faculty don't care about him as a person. The center, in effect, becomes the safety valve for the conscience of faculty who, because of increasing pressures to establish and maintain reputations in their specialties, have decreased their personal commitments to students.

Two seemingly contradictory sets of attitudes toward the center's individual counseling seem to be present among faculty and administrators: the center's principal value for some is its availability to handle student problems that distress staff members or require a special technique such as testing; for others like those mentioned above, the center is the agency to refer a student with any problem, thus freeing them from responsibility for interpersonal relationships with students. Neither role is adequate for a fully functioning center. In the former case, the center is being used as a back-up or emergency aid station for the counseling being conducted by staff who become involved with students, and, in the latter case, the center is being used as a substitute by staff who wish to avoid human contact with students.

The center can have more than a limited impact in providing individual counseling; however, the professional counselors must assume responsibility for sharing the skills and attitudes which are

65

essential for effective counseling with those in daily contact with students. They must work at minimizing the center's use as a buffer between faculty and the students who need personal contact with adults. At the same time, they must identify potential resource people and assist them to improve their effectiveness with students. For instance, when interested faculty and campus ministers make themselves available as draft and abortion counselors, the professional counselors can offer to discuss counseling procedures and to conduct practicum seminars.

Typically the professional counselors have ignored the existence of helping contacts between students and others on the campus. This passivity results in large measure from the attitude of professionals who self-consciously disassociate themselves from those without the appropriate degree, who may, however, be performing functions similar to their own. By disregarding the situation, they are not forced to take action. This attitude is reinforced by the feeling of disengagement from campus affairs generated by the isolation of the counseling cubicle. This point has been discussed in Chapter Four. It might simply be added that the traditional counselor role on campus has been a rather comfortable one.

The world of the counseling center has been created mostly by the staff. Only minimal evaluation of the agency's effectiveness has been required. While faculty perform in public and administrators preside over segments of the college and are accountable for their successes or failures to higher administrators and to the public, counselors have typically engaged in an activity protected from evaluation by confidentiality. They have thus been able to avoid the usual administrative accountability. Controls have been internal and geared to the sensitivities of the local staff. Evaluation of total center effectiveness has infrequently been a major concern of its staff counselors, who have more generally limited their sharing of information about their work to discussion of individual interviews or cases. The effectiveness of the center has been determined by the length of its waiting list. If students are willing to wait in line for counseling, the center must be doing an adequate job.

A major block to the modification of the center's approach

to individual counseling on campus is the "professional standards" syndrome inculcated through counselor preparation programs. After investing three to five years in learning counseling skills, the professional counselor is reluctant to relinquish his proprietary rights to individual counseling on campus. It is difficult for him to accept the possibility of achieving counseling goals through assisting others to improve and enrich the human qualities of their contacts with students. It is difficult for him to accept the sharing of those skills and attitudes which would permit others to handle more of the one- and two-contact cases which currently consume more than half of the center's counseling time. And it is difficult for him to accept the possibility that because he has survived a doctoral training program he may be less approachable by some segments of the student body and less sensitive to the problems of others (Carkhuff, 1969).

To maintain that individual counseling must be conducted only by those who have received official professional approval is unrealistic. A survey which I conducted covering twenty-one of the twenty-three counseling psychology programs approved by the Education and Training Board of the APA revealed that during one recent four-year period, 290 counseling psychologists had been graduated, with approximately 90 of this number going initially into college counseling centers. A companion survey of counseling centers in 56 major state colleges and universities indicated that they employed approximately 300 staff members with the doctorate. If these centers were staffed completely by counseling psychologists, the figures would indicate a fourteen-year production for the APA approved programs. Obviously, many of the doctoral personnel come from nonapproved programs and other professional backgrounds. A more comprehensive survey by Oetting (1970) indicated that 603 of the 1155 four-year colleges contacted reported formal counseling activities. Where there was a designated director, 303 held the doctorate and 85 did not. Of staff, 350 held the doctorate and 516 did not; 71 held only a bachelor's degree.

These figures indicate that the doctorates in counseling are concentrated in the major state schools. My survey of 56 major state colleges reveals only about 100 fewer staff doctorates than appear in Oetting's survey of 603 four-year colleges. Half of Oetting's colleges with formal counseling activities do not have a director with a doctorate and, except in the major colleges, if there are staff members other than the director, they are likely to be subdoctoral people. These figures emphasize that a substantial proportion of college counseling is being conducted by personnel who do not qualify as professional counselors by the doctoral degree standards set by the profession.

The issue of who is qualified to engage in individual counseling within a four-year college seems to be a moot question. Even within the official formal counseling services much counseling is carried on by less than fully qualified personnel. Once doctoral-level counselors can accept that there is a discrepancy between their ideal and reality, they may be able to view the imparting of their counseling knowledge to other nonprofessionals on campus with less alarm.

Figures from the APA approved counselor education programs suggest that the profession is producing relatively few "approved" counselors for college centers. Maintaining that the doctorate is the certificate of competency for engaging in individual counseling forces the profession into several logical extensions of this position. The first is that large numbers of college students, perhaps the majority, must by definition be relegated to receiving substandard counseling. The second is that we are apparently willing to accept counseling by substandard people when it serves our purpose, as can be seen in that all the clients used for practicum are handled by nondegreed trainees. Either we are cynical about our responsibilities to all clients or we do, in fact, believe that clients can benefit from contact with subdoctoral personnel. Thirdly, the doctorate from a counselor training program may mean different things depending on the interests and competencies of the particular individuals; nevertheless, we tend to use the degree as the certificate for competency in individual counseling. And, finally, approval of selected counselor education programs and internship facilities raises the question about the qualifications of those with the doctorate from nonapproved programs.

Professional Standards in Counselor Training

The contradictions which result from using the doctorate as the certificate of competency for engaging in individual counseling point up the problems in setting standards for the use of a particular technique in helping individuals. Setting standards for a particular type of service which are ideal rather than realistic can impair the public image of the profession by obscuring discriminations which professionals may be able to make but which are obscure or confusing to lay people. The profession may appear unresponsive to public needs or simply to be striving for a position of status. Legal counselors, used car counselors, fashion counselors and fifty-seven other varieties of counselors stand ready to help the public. The presence of doctoral-level counselors has little effect in enhancing the public image attached to the general term "counselor." That the public should be confused about the particular value of counselors with the doctorate might be expected since even within the profession we cannot—or will not—refine the term to the point where it differentiates the activities, skills, or special characteristics of counselors with the doctorate from those of other counselors—or from clinical psychologists. One way of enhancing the image of counselors trained to the doctoral level has been to draw on the alleged status of clinical psychology, arguing that counselors and clinicians are basically indistinguishable when their therapy cases are analyzed. This strategy has simply complicated the question of what is unique in the doctoral-level counselor's repertoire.

I have already discussed the fact that much of what the counselor does in regard to individual contacts with students is indistinguishable to many on the college campus from what a variety of other personnel do. College counseling centers average from two to three contacts per case and a significant proportion of the clients are seen only once. It would seem that the doctoral-level counselor may be overtrained for many of the individual contact functions he is now performing. When only a small proportion of center cases continue beyond three or four contacts, it is reasonable to ask whether a counselor requires several years of graduate work and a research dissertation to be considered capable of coping with the student problems currently being handled in the college center.

69

New Myths and Old Realities

The counselor trained to the doctorate has a role to perform in the counseling center, but he is currently being used very inefficiently if he devotes the largest proportion of his time to individual contacts with clients. A doctoral program in counseling provides the counselor with a broad base in psychological theory and a wide range of skills for research, educational-vocational guidance, personal counseling, and group leadership. On the other hand, it also encourages an attitude of possessiveness which may boost his ego but which is unrealistic in light of the actual campus situation. As budgets tighten and student populations grow, the center staff will be involved with a diminishing proportion of individual contacts with students while various forms of counseling with the bulk of the student body will continue to be conducted by personnel unqualified by professional standards.

Individual and group counseling are important parts of the college's services to students, but these services need to be available to a larger proportion of the student body than the doctoral-level counselors can hope to reach personally. Doctoral-level personnel should, of course, be available for working with students having serious emotional upsets and for diagnosing cases for referral, but they should not become heavily involved in individual case contacts.

For the professional counselor to have any significant impact on the individual and group counseling services to students, his primary task will have to be training, supervision and consultation. He will need to work with faculty, administrators, and older students in the settings where individual and group contacts with students normally take place, such as residence halls, living groups, advisors' offices, placement services, and financial aid offices. The role of the professional counselor will be to make available his skills and understanding of psychological and counseling processes to improve the quality of human relationships where they occur naturally and spontaneously. When some special counseling skills or techniques are needed (educational-vocational testing or an emotional crisis), students can be referred to the counseling center. As is already being done in captive training centers, the bulk of the counseling in the center would be conducted by subdoctoral staff trained and closely supervised by senior staff. Unlike the captive agency, however, these support personnel would not be enrolled in a doctoral program but rather terminal M.A. level counselors, instructional staff working part time in the center, or college-educated housewives.

The model on which professional counseling has developed has been that of the clinician—direct remedial service to individual clients. This model is in need of radical modification if the profession is to be effective in the society and remain a meaningful entity. This modification is particularly critical for the college campus. Theoretically, the doctoral-trained counselor is prepared to understand human relationship problems and to perform a variety of functions. In devoting the major share of his time to contacts with individuals in the center, the professional counselor restricts himself to the use of a fraction of his total potential, and this with an insignificant segment of the student population. The clinical model is remedial in nature and, by definition, limited in application. The model most appropriate to professional counseling is based on human strengths, individual differences and normal development (Tyler, 1961). To be effective and efficient in operating within this model, the counselor does well to divest himself of much of his remedial work while assisting others to perform this function more adequately and devoting more of his time and energy to activities of general impact on campus. An additional benefit to the counselor moving out of his office would be his becoming an integral part of the campus community and receiving the feed-back necessary for increasing his potential contributions to that community.

The goal of the center staff should be to assist other parts of the institution in humanizing the educational and administrative processes for students. No other group of personnel is as free to undertake this task. The student personnel staff is theoretically engaged in this enterprise, but the very nature of their responsibilities to the central administration reduces (sometimes to zero) whatever personal effectiveness they may, as individuals, wish to have with students and faculty. Counseling center staff on the other hand are in a generally ambiguous position and viewed by students and faculty as posing little, if any, threat. They can, therefore, be more critical, encouraging or confronting without raising suspicions about their ulterior motivations.

There are two major problems to be overcome before professional counselors can move toward implementing the proposed role. The first of these is the preparation for such a role and the second is its acceptance on campus. The second tends to flow from the first. The doctoral-level counselor, oriented toward a more flexible role while proceeding through his training program, is likely to try more effective activities on the job. The counselor oriented in his training program primarily toward individual counseling and private research is not likely to view one of his functions as stimulating a market for a wider range of services, or of breaking down his functions into those components which can be taught to others. Others on campus do not automatically look to the counseling center as a resource for assistance with problems related to advising and interpersonal relationships. The professional staff must sensitize the campus to the consulting and training services they are equipped and willing to offer. This requires personal contacts with individuals who may be ready to institute pilot programs or to become involved in in-service training groups. If these pilot projects are successful, the demand will follow for an expansion of the service. The counseling center, as pointed out in Chapter One, has generally been assigned (or accepted) a stereotypical role on campus. This "place to send kids with vocational or personal problems" role will not be modified unless the counselors take the initiative in showing willingness to share their special knowledge about such things as interpersonal relations, and normal development with others, and in proving their value as active participants in the campus change process.

Most fundamental to any modification of the role for the professional counselor is a revision of current counselor preparation programs. The first step is a chauvinistic one: the profession must stop playing Charley Brown and proceed on the proposition that it is a membership of people with a unique combination of practice skills and academic background who can perform novel and distinctive functions. Counseling preparation cannot be adulterated clinical preparation and serve the needs of a unique professional group. Unless a distinctive, meaningful curriculum is designed to achieve specific goals, counseling at the doctoral level will disappear. It needs, perhaps, to disappear, but as a conscious transformation rather than as the result of being slowly absorbed by several other specialties.

Concentration on individual counseling techniques is extremely limiting to the counselor. The flight into administration or counselor education programs out of counseling service positions is one indication of dissatisfaction with the present unstimulating role. The counselor education program, rather than remaining static in its current conceptualization of producing skilled individual counselors, must be revamped to allow its graduates to move easily and confidently into a variety of active roles in a range of settings. The counselor should be prepared to seek out situations in which he can apply his special skills rather than to simply sit in his office and interact with clients.

The curriculum of the program must be designed from the current and anticipated needs of the settings in which professional counselors are most likely to be hired. The curriculum offerings must be predicated on the assumption that these needs can best be assessed by direct feed-back from the service agency settings. This is a reversal of the usual flow of information which has traditionally moved from the educational setting to the service setting. Consultants have ordinarily moved out of educational settings to help service agencies with their problems or to oversee the internships in those settings. Realistically, consultants should be moving in both directions, with service personnel attending the curriculum meetings of the educational staff, and even assisting with the teaching of courses in the educational facility. What is most needed in the educational program is a broadening of service possibilities rather than a narrowing to the counseling specialty.

What is being done in the professional field? What are the possibilities for service by professionals with our interests and capabilities? These should be the questions asked as the curriculum is

73

revised. For the counselor with the doctorate working in the college setting, it seems that underlying all of his practical work is a concentration on the multitude of problems facing higher education, an understanding of the teacher-learner process, a firm grasp of the "late adolescent period," a background in group processes, and an appreciation of minority group problems, particularly as they relate to the college. These are essential learnings for someone who plans to work in a college setting, therefore they should take precedence over a concentration on the theoretical and practical aspects of clinical work. The emphasis should be placed on helping essentially normal students become more effective and in helping parts of the institution define goals and modify programs for the benefit and well-being of students. On the applied level, the program needs greater emphasis on working with others to help them do a more effective job in their individual and group contacts with students. Basically, any program of education for counselors at the doctoral level must be both flexible to meet the needs of individual students and fluid to meet the changing requirements of the organizations and institutions in which the counselors will work. The program, furthermore, should incorporate the means to help those enrolled in the program to evaluate themselves as persons and to gain confidence in their ability to operate independently as consultants and social agents in the organization for which they will work.

The graduates of such a training program should be prepared to have their work evaluated publicly, as differentiated from the private evaluation of single clients. They must be prepared, in other words, to carry out activities which can be seen by a variety of people and to be evaluated by those people. Their research, for instance, will be action research and have implications beyond the counseling room. It will not be designed simply to share with other professionals through journal publication but rather to bring about change in or have an impact on the institution. Thus, it will be open to critical scrutiny by those whom the research may affect.

The strength of the program for professional counselors will be in its flexibility and response to consumer needs. The body of knowledge would be broad and interdisciplinary. Technique courses would be deemphasized or eliminated with the now unrelated units in occupational information, educational-vocational testing, and counseling techniques absorbed into on-the-job practicums. Projective techniques and testing courses aimed at preparing test administrators would be eliminated from the program. Internships in psychiatric hospitals would be used only in those unusual cases where they contributed to the future goals of specific trainees. Those planning to become college counselors should not ordinarily be assigned to hospital internships. Except for those planning to work in a mental hospital, internships would not be designed to develop therapy skills with emotionally disturbed patients but simply to add substance to the course work in abnormal psychology. The rationale that V.A. and other medical internships are necessary for the financial support of counselor trainees should be rejected and greater effort made to find sources of support and placement in nonmedical agencies similar to those in which the graduates will eventually be employed. Smooth-working relationships with academic advisors, deans and student groups are not learned in the hospital setting. The contention that APA approval for internships should be a prerequisite to the placement of a trainee is unacceptable as virtually all approved agencies are medically (therapy) oriented, thus counselors are seduced by financial pressures into situations totally irrelevant in philosophical orientation to the settings in which many trainees will be employed. The profession has allowed itself to be lured into the worst sort of education-by-expediency through its acceptance of financial support for trainees as a major determinant of its internship placements.

One result of this reliance on expediency has been to confuse the counselor about his basic service model and, almost as importantly, to waste his valuable training time by preventing him from working in settings more appropriate to his future position. The current policy works a particular hardship on college counseling center directors who are too often faced with applicants who have hospital internships, but little, if any, counseling center experience. There is no excuse for this situation. Serious questions have been raised about APA approval of programs and internships, and rightly so. The entire approval system needs to be reevaluated as there is something wrong with a system in which significant numbers of doctoral-level counselors aspire to positions in college counseling centers while only a few centers on college campuses have been approved as training centers.

Internships are available in college counseling centers; however, many of these are in captive agencies and relatively little "trading around" of interns goes on. As a result, the new counselor, even if he has experience in a center, often has been supervised by the same faculty from whom he has taken his course work. His experiences are generally limited to one familiar environment. The profession is well advised to encourage placement in centers other than those attached to the academic program in which the student has taken his course work and to facilitate distant placement through travel grant awards.

When individual counseling is the major focus of the educational experience of the professional counselor, the practicum and internship locale may be of secondary importance. However, if an ability to cope with a variety of situations and an awareness of the range of possible services offered by counselors, not to mention an appreciation of different administrative styles, are to be important learnings of the practicum-internship period, then these practical experiences should be encouraged in situations relevant to the trainee's major vocational goal. They certainly should not be restricted to captive agencies or medical settings simply because of stipend availability.

The purpose of counselor education should parallel that of counseling itself: increasing the student's awareness of the range of possibilities open to him, helping him to work through the alternatives, making the student more aware of himself and his strengths, and encouraging the student to act in and on the environment. Most importantly, the program should be patterned to fit each student's needs and style. We reject the concept of a preplanned package with limited goals in our counseling with clients; we should reject a preplanned package with limited goals in our preparation of counselors.

Vocational
Development
Counseling

SIX

As college counseling center staff undertake different roles within the campus community, traditionalists within and outside the center will inevitably raise the question: "What happens to vocational counseling?" As indicated in Chapter One, the college counseling center is rooted in the veterans' placement service. The concept that young people need only a few tests and a bit of guidance from an adult to settle them into a vocational channel is deeply embedded in the thinking of an older generation which faced relatively few choices and considerably less complexity within occupational fields.

The concept is related to two beliefs within our society: there is one optimum choice to be made from any set of alternatives, and a concise answer is possible to any problem if enough data can be accumulated. More recently, perhaps due to radio and TV program time limitations, we have developed an infinite faith in the possibility of instantaneous solutions for the most intricate problems. The first belief leads a man to look for the one and only woman to be his wife, a student to search for the one answer to an exam question, a housewife to assume that there is one best floorwax or scouring powder, and almost everyone to seek for the work slot designed just for him. Belief number two is self-explanatory; Americans have a deep conviction that any problem can be solved successfully if enough facts are available. We have become increasingly a computer society. A machine now absorbs and regurgitates data in a few hours which would have taken a dedicated researcher a lifetime to collect and analyze. And, finally, we want our problems solved and questions answered immediately. We are not a patient people and distrust those who point out the contradictions and discontinuities on the way to any goal. We prefer to ignore the past and to use the present as our base for decisions about the future.

The implications for vocational guidance seem obvious. We have emphasized procedures which rely on quick, simple data collection and feed-back. A short talk at Career Day by someone in the job, a one- or two-page description of an occupation, a few scores or profiles from tests, and answers flashed on a TV screen by a computer. These are the core of vocational guidance. No one would suggest that decisions should be made in vacuum. "Don't confuse me with the facts" is hardly an adequate motto for making rational decisions about one's future plans, but facts alone are not enough.

The issue is not one of information input as opposed to no information input but rather the priorities which are assigned to data gathering during the process. To take a ludicrous example: explaining to a first grade youngster the difference between a chemist and a physicist or between a clinical psychologist and a social case worker would be an exercise in futility. The first grader, even if he were sophisticated enough to comprehend the nuances, is certainly not at a stage in his own development to perceive meaning for himself in the information given to him. Child psychologists know better than I what types of learning have meaning to a first grader, but I am certain that only gross vocational information about the first grader's immediate experiential world are of interest or usefulness to him.

By the time the young person reaches eighth or ninth grade, he is faced with choices about his future educational direction. He may have to choose between a foreign language or band, between shop or a writing class, between American history or math. At this point, some sort of vocational guidance enters his life in the form of suggestions from parents, teachers or guidance personnel. Unless one or another of these adults is sensitive to the meaning of these choices for future educational possibilities, the chances are good that the youngster may begin to reduce his degrees of freedom for future choices without any awareness of the implications of what he is doing. Generally, the decisions the eighth or ninth graders make are a mixture of general interest in what the subject seems to be about, the reputation of the teacher to whom he will be bound, the prejudices of the parents and teachers who give him advice and, perhaps most importantly, the reactions of the student group with which he most closely identifies.

The process involves a significant amount of personal, also irrational, response to present situational factors. The interpretation he gives to test scores at this point is most probably in proportion to how closely they match the picture he has of himself in relation to interpersonal groupings within the school rather than a future occupational goal. For instance, if he sees himself as one of the athletic group, the "outdoor" on the Kuder will be rationalized into this context. Through high school and his college or work years, the young person is trying to make sense out of himself and what his role in relation to others should be. Certainly rationality enters into the data collection in which he engages formally and informally but, despite the adult society's desire for him to be efficient in his search for the educational-vocational goal best suited to him, his emotional inclination is to avoid being channeled and slotted.

The young person, partially in response to his parents' fear that he won't find his self-supporting niche and his teachers' concerns that his floundering may be a reflection on their educational capabilities, will go along with the indicators laid out for him by adults. He will choose courses, schools or jobs which the significant adults in his environment encourage him to consider. It is the adults who insist on practicality and efficiency aimed at the future. The young person is still embroiled through high school and early work or college years in a search, a search for meanings for himself in the things he is doing. Some can relate future occupational goals to this search but many can not. To be able to relate an occupation to oneself in a meaningful way requires first that one know and understand oneself. Few young people have more than the most tentative notions about who they are.

It is at this point where vocational guidance of the traditional sort breaks down. Its emphasis on cross-sectional information about a few characteristics of the student (interests, personality, and values as measured by paper and pencil tests) and some information about jobs (working conditions, salaries, and usual activities) is inadequate to the needs which have the highest priority for the late adolescent. Are your interests more like successful people in business than like successful people in science? Do you have higher interests in social service than clerical activities as measured by this test? Do you admire Einstein or Shakespeare more? These may be pertinent questions in clarifying some things which the young person probably knows about himself, but it is only with an incredible leap of faith that one can tie test scores into the choice of a specific occupation three, five, or ten years in the future with any degree of confidence. The best that can be hoped is that the short time in which a counselor talks with a student and the few test scores he has available will allow the student to consider some broad general field within the vast occupational world. If he is lucky, the test results may raise questions about himself that he hadn't considered before.

With little real experience in testing himself out in the working world, the young person is asked to make more and more specific decisions affecting his future role as a worker at an earlier and earlier point in his life. The adult demands for better vocational guidance are directed at a situation in which young people whom they have increasingly cut off from meaningful interactions with all but an educational process are quite naturally confused about where they can fit into a complex and continually changing and unknown future. And this during a period when the student's grasp of who he is and what is really most important to him is likely to be extremely disorganized.

To further complicate matters for the young person is a shift in the attitudes of large numbers of his peers toward the concept of work itself. Many young people are questioning the work ethic in which a man's value is determined by the current status society ascribes to the job which he is doing. As the pressure builds from adults to increase the efficiency with which students are slotted into educational channels aimed at specific jobs and careers, a counterpressure is building among youth to increase their options, to increase the meaning of their current activities for the lives they are living in the present. The students call it "relevance," but by whatever term it is called it means that a growing number of young people want more from life than the rat race in which they see their parents engaged.

Reality for adults may be improved guidance to assist youth to make earlier decisions about their future. Reality for young people is an existential search for meaning in present events and present relationships, not a meaning tied to a future occupation which may not even exist by the time they are ready to enter the job market. This is the alienation which I perceive in the adolescents who come to the counseling center. The utopias, shangri-las, and jerusalems which have motivated their parents' generation have been destroyed. While adults may swell with pride at the planting of a plastic American flag on the moon, many of their sons and daughters view the event as merely an astronaut's ego-trip. The pleasure and joy that was supposed to come with affluence, two cars in the garage of a split-level house in the green suburbs, has been very sporadic and temporary. For many young people the advantages of affluence have been bought at the price of harried fathers who hate their work, bored mothers, and often completely splintered family relationships. They are asking in the words of a recent popular ballad: "Is that all there is?"

It is not my intention to repeat the lengthy list of factors which place young people in an entirely different relationship to their society and the world than any other group of young Americans has faced before, but a few of the more obvious are the literal killing of our environment in order to support a technological society, the ever-present potential of exterminating all of mankind, the incredible geographical mobility of our population, and the continuing disappearance of entire occupational groups and major realignments or modifications of others. Young people are witnessing thousands of professionals and high-level technicians losing their employment because of changes in national policies and other thousands laid off as a sacrifice to the government's desire to slow down inflation. Any one of these things might in itself make long-range planning for a future vocational position extremely risky. Coping with the implications of these and other very substantial threats to predicting the future might be expected to have exactly the effects on young people that they are having.

Some are simply ignoring the possibility of any discontinuities in what has been accepted by the established adult society as progress toward a form of perfect society. These students study, select courses, and plan for future job placement as if they could rely on the stability of their environment. Others are swept by despair and drop out or retreat through drugs or isolated rural communes. Still others approach each situation and relationship in a tentative manner, planning only so far as seems practical for that event or interaction. Obviously, any attempt at categorization is open to question, but it seems that vocational planning as most adults view the process can be entered into seriously by most young people only by an extreme narrowing or distortion of their perceptions. Those who are willing to plan on the basis of current occupational literature and test information must do so on an "as if" basis, accepting the data as if they will have relevance for a specific action four, six, or ten years in the future.

Planning on an "as if" basis would be a perfectly natural approach to projections into the future except that adults tend to transform the whole process into a series of irrevocable commitments, and soon the young person finds himself locked into a system which is very unforgiving of mistakes and miscalculations. The adolescent who decides to take a course because his friends are enrolled in that class may neglect, because of a time conflict, to take some other course which he later discovers is a prerequisite to a sequence of courses which he needs in order to be accepted at a college he wants to attend. That may mean he is prevented from entering a program he had wanted to take at that college, which in turn may close the door to an occupational specialty he could have successfully pursued. One might argue that with better vocational guidance the student should have been persuaded that he was closing a door to his future by not taking the courses he needed. The student probably feels at the time he decides to take the course in which his friends are enrolled that being with friends is the most important factor in his life at that particular point in his development. A freshman college student may transfer to a less desirable school in which his fiancee is enrolled. If they break up, the move may be seen as foolish in retrospect, but at the time the decision was made, the couple's need to spend considerable amounts of time together may have been the most important factor in their lives at that point in their general development. Vocational counseling can be effective only to the extent that it can incorporate the student's current developmental priorities. Otherwise it will be a technique for manipulation or coercion of young people by adults.

Most of us must operate on an "as if" basis in order to maintain our psychological stability, but the heavy use of drugs and alcohol and the mass hypnotism of spectator sports and TV viewing seem to give some indication of the difficulty with which Americans face the reality of their lives. Professionals who are considered experts in helping young people plan for their future jobs or careers are in a particularly difficult position. They are being asked to justify their value on the basis of their ability to slot accurately and effectively—to move students through the educational process with as little disruption to the system as possible. The high school guidance personnel have, until recently, perceived their status as being tied to the proportion of their students whom they could successfully enroll in four-year colleges. Annual reports of high school guidance offices have featured a list of seniors and the colleges to which they have been admitted. The college counseling center has typically devoted a major share of its time to educational-vocational counseling of the traditional test intepretation variety; however, as staff members have become better trained and more sophisticated, they have tended to shift emphasis from the placement aspects of the process inherent in occupational information and test results to assisting the student explore himself in relation to his past and present environment, helping him to answer questions such as: "What kind of a person am I? What types of relationships are important to me? What kinds of things do I need to take into account in making decisions about my life?" rather than the more superficial questions related to fitting his tested characteristics to future occupational possibilities.

If my evaluation of the situation above has any validity, this self-exploration makes more common sense and certainly makes much more psychological sense than the past stress on matching the person's present characteristics as evaluated by paper and pencil tests of dubious predictive value in individual cases with already outdated job descriptions. The fact that this match is to take place at an indefinite time in the future within the context of a continually shifting and increasingly uncertain job market makes the process highly questionable. However, the process does have one feature which makes it attractive to the American public: there are scores, figures and quantities involved. Whether a score or colored bar on a graph has any actual validity means very little to most

Americans; it has an appearance of concreteness and this in itself conveys the aura of value. This attitude is exemplified by an incident involving a doctoral candidate in a student personnel administration program who came to the counseling center to ask about some personality test which he might administer to a group of students. Neither the experienced psychometrist nor I had ever heard of the instrument. This potential dean of students, who will most likely be making decisions affecting the counseling center at an institution of higher education in the near future, looked a bit glum and remarked: "Gee, that's too bad. We used it at Far Out College when I was an assistant dean of men there, and it gives real neat profiles."

This faith in scores or graphs as having some meaning would be amusing except that in the absence of genuinely meaningful data the young person who has little confidence in himself or his own decision-making capabilities will seize on those abstract numbers, shaded bars and pointed profiles as revealed truth about himself. They become him. He will read occupational literature, although most of it will bore him to tears, as if that job will remain that job six years from the date he is reading the information. Having few internal resources for making decisions and being pressured by friends, relatives, and society to have a goal, the high school senior or college freshman seizes these few pieces of data he can see as a reflection of himself and a tangible future and he chooses, with some encouraging or discouraging interpretations of the data by his vocational counselor. The less sophisticated the counselor about the world of work and human development, the greater his investment in this potentially disillusioning charade. The counselor who has been trained as a technician (the one-term NDEA retreads, for instance) is more likely to share the student's desire to have something tangible to grasp and, hence, his greater reliance on tests as diagnostic instruments, superficial self-reports of historical data and occupational information.

The greater the understanding of the counselor about the inherent difficulty that many students face in making decisions about the future because of the fluid situation in which they are growing up and, equally as important, because they have had little opportunity to explore their values, attitudes and interests in reality situations outside the school, the more likely he is to concentrate on firming up the student's self-concept. He may use tests, but as a "talking device" rather than diagnostic or predictive instruments. His approach to the student is that of encouraging self-exploration, for he knows that if, in fact, an occupation is chosen as an expression of self-concept, the person must be clear as to what his self-concept is. The goal of counseling is to assist the student to learn how to use knowledge about himself in making decisions and to increase his degrees of freedom, for the counselor knows that, where all parts of the environment are in flux, the critical problem for the young person is to learn how to cope with an ever-changing situation whenever he is forced to make some decision. This is the opposite of the stereotypical, vocational guidance approach where the goal is the narrowing of choices and the keying in on some specific future objective.

The difference may, on the surface, seem relatively minor, but in terms of the counselor's attitude toward the client and toward the goal he is attempting to reach, it makes a world of difference. Unfortunately, it also has the effect of making evaluation of results virtually impossible, except as a follow-up of a student seen by a counselor indicates that the feelings of that student about himself and his situation have improved in directions indicated by the counselor's predictions about his future. There is no simple matching of test results and future educational or vocational choice, for instance. Nor are there those old standbys of improved grades or the decrease of attrition, for it is not only conceivable, but quite possible, that good counseling will result in a lessening of the pressures which an individual student feels to measure his accomplishment by grade point averages or to remain in an uncomfortable and unprofitable school situation.

Disturbingly those in positions to support counseling are, without the slightest doubt, going to demand direct relationships between counseling and such measurable items as higher grades, lower attrition, and lessened drop-and-add requests. Those who support counseling can be expected to do so on the basis of more efficient slotting and channeling rather than higher student mobility and greater reluctance to commit themselves to specific decisions. And that is the crux of one of the major problems facing counseling: its goals are, or should be, diametrically opposite to the demands which the traditionalists and the so-called establishment want them to be. Elsewhere in this book, I have indicated how vulnerable the counseling center is and how dependent is its survival on the good will of those in power within the institutional administration. Therefore, I have no easy answer to this obvious conflict of goals which puts the professional counselor in confrontation with his major sources of support. It is a problem to which the profession must address itself or see its high-sounding and idealistic purposes corrupted in practice as a matter of expediency to assure the counseling center's survival.

Events in our society and the world in general are moving with inhuman rapidity. Professional counseling, particularly as it has been engaged in educational-vocational choice, is in a crisis period. It appears close to obsolescence, even before it has produced the results it was touted as capable of producing during those giddy years when NDEA was pouring thousands of guidance people into the schools and hundreds of doctorates back into the process of training more guidance personnel. Few raised objections to this mass production of teacher retreads, but the disillusionment with their ability to do what society, as expressed through federal grant encouragement, expected of them has resulted in a dramatic reduction of support for the continued training of these traditionally programmed counselors.

The need for a complete revamping of the professional counselor's approach to the vocational decision making of young people can be illustrated by reference to ethnic minorities and women. The relationship of these groups to the world of work is in a period of rapid transformation. The counselor's traditional techniques are of limited value in working with other than Caucasian males. When occupations require college or graduate education, the counselor has discovered that normative data for tests as well as his own experience restricts his already limited ability to diagnose and predict to Caucasian middle-class males. Minorities have been correct in their objection to the use of the usual prediction and selection devices in making judgments about their capabilities. Significant numbers of minority students will not use the services of the college counseling center because their contacts with secondary school guidance personnel have been uniformly negative and discouraging. I have no exact figures, but my experience leads me to believe that almost all minority students who enter college have done so in spite of the evidence presented to them by guidance personnel that they had no chance of success. Several black graduate students with whom I have talked have been bitter about and contemptuous of the counseling which they have received. They perceive counselors as "the enemy" rather than helpers.

The statement of the college counselor whom I have quoted elsewhere in another context that: "My main job is defeating the predictions" is particularly true as the heterogeneity of the college student body increases. However, I would add that another task for the counselor is to broaden the concept of prediction to include a variety of other more individualized factors than those now in use while limiting the scope of prediction to immediate and short-term outcomes. The counselor must look for special skills and signs of motivation which allow him to encourage the minority student to attempt the next step in his educational or vocational development. He must resist closing out opportunities simply because the traditional grade point and test predictors do not show promise of the successful completion of some activity a year or two in the future.

Ethnic minorities are not in college-level occupations in sufficient numbers to allow us to make more than very generalized predictions of the potential for any particular member of these groups to succeed. One goal of the counselor is that of assisting blacks, chicanos, American Indians, and other members of under-represented minority groups to work through their feelings about competing with the dominant Caucasian males. There is little in the background or training of the professional counselor other than his own sensitivity which gives him the resources to cope with those people who probably for the next decade or longer will be pioneering in occupational fields previously closed to them.

Ethnic minorities are particularly sensitive to what they perceive as the lack of understanding by professional counselors of the particular problems resulting from their being discriminated against and disadvantaged during their lifetime. There is no doubt that a serious communication barrier exists between the middle-class professional counselor and the ethnic minority student. Fundamentally, counseling in its traditional form is a middle-class invention set in the formal trappings of waiting room, receptionist, applications, appointments, ties and jackets, and a lengthy verbal exchange between an authority figure, no matter how sympathetic he may be personally, and someone who offers himself in a dependent posture. These factors would be enough to deter most ethnic minority students from using the regular counseling service. Going to the counseling center for assistance of any sort, especially when the counselor is a white male, is like coming out of the field with hat in hand to see THE MAN. There is little doubt that the center will reach few minority students if the counselors do not move out of their offices. This has recently been the experience in one college situation with which I am familiar. The counselor in this particular case is a member of a minority group. Freshman minority students were requested to meet with her individually once a week in the center to talk over their academic and personal problems. Some did come, but reluctantly, and she was able to make contact with the rest only when she met with them on a more unscheduled basis in the residence halls and other places where they tended to hang out.

But these physical barriers are only a part of the obstacle to communication. If a counselor is fortunate enough, as I have been, to spend some time with a professional black counselor who is willing to demonstrate the differences in verbal and body language between whites and blacks, it will quickly become apparent that many of the characteristic gestures and word usages of the black are quite incomprehensible to the whites, while common reactions of white professionals are viewed as put-downs or status reinforcers by

89

the blacks. The black student and the white professional may converse using English words and yet be talking completely different languages. The white will be receiving only very carefully screened messages but will be unintentionally sending out negative communications which reinforce the distance between himself and the black student. At present I feel white professional counselors may act as advisors to minority students in regard to the system or the institutional structure, but very few are capable of acting as effective counselors.

In the case of women, the situation so far as counseling is concerned is a somewhat different matter. By and large, women seem more accepting of counseling than men, perhaps because they are accustomed to the dominant-submissive roles inherent in the counseling situation. In some ways, this very fact is symbolic of the major difficulty in working with women on vocational planning. The relationship beween the sexes is being challenged by some women, but the legacy of deferring to males and perceiving themselves as subordinates is very strong, even among the more career-oriented women. This is not to say that a particular woman client may not firmly insist on her independence and her desire for equality but rather that it is difficult for a woman who has learned automatic dependency and submission responses to males through every facet of her development to break through these response patterns and act on her own strengths with a true sense of self. She has difficulty in acting rather than simply reacting to male leads.

The professional counselor is in a position of dominance, not only because the counseling relationship encourages that set but also because the counselor is probably a man. The woman client is in a sense confronted with working on her attitudes toward men, her ambitions and needs outside the usual homemaking role, her feelings about potential discrimination and other topics related to her role in society with one of the enemy in a setting which tends to highlight the inequality of the participants. The counselor's attitudes toward women and their roles become very much a factor in whether or not the counselor will be able to assist the woman student overcome, at least partially, the learning experiences which predispose her toward a passive-dependent approach to men and the world of work which they dominate.

The counselor who has traditional attitudes toward women, seeing them primarily as sex objects, homemakers and child raisers, is unlikely to be able to handle the conflicts within the woman who has even a minimal interest in meeting her needs for meaning and accomplishment outside the home. If he has fears about pressures from his own wife to move beyond her traditional homemaking activities, he can quickly extinguish a female client's explorations of her needs to be something other than a wife and mother. In some ways, for a male counselor to be an effective vocational counselor for a woman, he may have to be something of a traitor to his own sex and encourage the woman to attack the sources of domination within his own sexual attitudes. Before the female client can make any progress in examining her basic feelings about using her skills, talents and intelligence in the working world, she will first have to go through the anxieties which any client experiences when she finds herself in opposition to the prevailing cultural expectations. The counselor who has concern about his own relationship with women is likely to respond unconsciously to the cues which he will receive from almost all women about their ambivalence to the work-home-making question in ways which encourage the more traditional attitudes expressed by the woman. It is much easier for him to reinforce her traditional attitudes toward women's roles than to support her tentative explorations of need fulfillment outside marriage and a family.

If the male counselor is uncomfortable with other than traditional relationships with women, he will have difficulty in working with strong, capable, intelligent women who have clear non-traditional vocational goals. A counselor who can confront an aggressive male client with assurance and positive regard, using the client's strengths as a base for discussion of suitable vocational outlets, may feel completely put down by a strong woman client. It is not unusual for him to dismiss the female client as lacking the feminine qualities she will need to succeed or to make attempts to move her case into a personal problem category, apparently figuring

he has to straighten out her aggression problem if she is to be successful in the occupational world.

Problems facing ethnic minorities and women in vocational
decision making highlight the complications facing counselors in
their attempts to assist college students with educational-vocational
choice. Vocational guidance has never really been a simple task,
even though the availability of easily administered and scored test
instruments and ample occupational literature has given this activity
a surface appearance of consisting of little more than automatic procedures. Vocational guidance has often been sloughed off to the less
well-trained counselors while those with the doctorate reserved their
time for more serious problems. The fact that neither ethnic minorities nor women can be given adequate vocational counseling employ-
ing the usual methods and techniques should bring into focus the
limitations in the vocational guidance that counselors have been
doing with the usual case load of white middle-class males.

Whether professional counseling will be able to take advantage of this threat to its established practices is uncertain. A great
many people have an investment in continuing to operate as they
have since World War II and the more recent NDEA years. Moreover, a pressure is building among administrators to "improve" vocational counseling, but the rationale for such improvement runs
counter to those values which vocational counselors should maintain in relation to the students with whom they work.

In these days of tight budgets and a sagging job market, the
press is for greater efficiency in selecting and directing young people
through the educational system to a specific job slot. Unfortunately
there are no truly efficient procedures for helping young people
discover themselves and find a meaningful and significant relationship to the world in which they live. Improving methods to grind
them through a mechanical vocational decision-making process like
sausages, with little regard for the primacy of their search for self,
can result only in frustration for the student and disillusionment
for the administrators who seem to expect that, with the proper
gimmicks and hardware, we will be able to shoot youngsters through

the school system into their proper vocational slots as accurately as we blast our astronauts to specific craters on the moon.

Professional counseling must make a commitment to the humane use of human beings or stand accused of the manipulation of the young for the benefit of technological efficiency.

Counseling and Student Personnel

SEVEN

A recent article by Penney (1968) concludes: "The long-sought 'profession' of student personnel work has not been, is not, and will not be recognized or accepted as a vital aspect of the academic world." For better or worse, the counseling service agency is generally a part of the student personnel administration; therefore, Penney's bleak view of the professional legitimacy of student personnel work must be of concern to professional counselors. Do we break loose from what appears to some to be an unsuccessful attempt to professionalize a disparate group of administrators? Do we declare our independence on the basis that we are not administrators and that counseling does have an accumulated body of knowledge and a specialized set of skills? Do we ignore the issue and hope for the best? Or should we assist in a reformulation of the entire area, recognizing that the potential goals of student personnel, as differentiated from its current operational activities, are compatible with those of professional counseling on the college campus?

As I read Penney, I hear him saying that student personnel cannot receive academic approval because its body of knowledge is borrowed from a variety of other more basic disciplines and therefore does not meet the criteria of a profession in this age of specialization and expertise. One result is that specialists are usurping the roles formerly played by student personnel workers. If Penney is narrowly defining "student personnel worker" as deans and sub-deans, his argument has validity, but recent trends seem to indicate that as the specialists take over housing, the union programming, foreign student advising, and so forth, the deans have moved up the administrative ladder to become managers of the business and personnel affairs of these specialty areas. Few deans of students in larger institutions have any more than ritual contacts with student groups, but they remain busy manipulating budgets and approving or disapproving requests from their service bureaus. At one university, a survey of student information about service and administrative personnel revealed that only 7 per cent of the student sample (fairly well distributed as to sex and living group affiliation) could identify the dean of students and less than 15 per cent could identify the associate deans. If these figures are at all typical, then one can certainly raise the question of whether students are any longer the main constituents of deans' offices. Since the graduate preparation of student personnel workers centers in those courses related to adolescent development, counseling and the problems of college students, the job activities of deans do not appear to be consonant with their "professional" preparation.

The bureaucratic structure of the modern institution of higher education does not permit loose agencies within its structure; therefore, it is unlikely that any counseling center will have the option of becoming independent. The trend appears to be one of greater centralization with the lines of responsibility clear and distinct. This means less freedom for individual units. Legislatures are making more direct decisions for the colleges through their budget control of an increasing number of line items; presidents or boards are directly controlling more of the programming of the college by shifting funds from one unit to another (as position vacancies occur or as money in certain accounts is not expended by some specific mid-year date, for instance); and schools within universities are reassigning faculty from low student contact courses to those in greater demand. Given the current financial crisis in education which is resulting in tighter central control, there is little reason to believe that a counseling center will be able to disaffiliate from its student personnel connections. As a relatively high cost service, professional counseling services are in an extremely vulnerable position during this depression period in higher education and more than ever before need to be integrated into a comprehensive student services structure.

It follows that the counseling center has a stake in assisting the SP administrative system to work well for the good of the greatest number of students. The current confusions within student personnel, therefore, are a threat to professional counselors who will need strong support for the work which they are doing on campus. It is in the interest of counseling centers that they assist the student services area with which they are most closely identified to define itself in terms which are meaningful to students, faculty, and the central administration. Does this sound presumptuous? I think not. In counseling, when the client is having identity problems and exhibits clear discontinuities between parts of his developmental history, the counselor assists him in clarifying his goals and his relationships with others. When the client's current activities are inconsistent with his professed value system, his efforts to reconcile the differences increase his own tensions and impair his relationships with others. Part of the counseling process requires that the counselor help the client to perceive himself as others perceive him rather than simply through his own distortions.

The gap between professed emphasis on the needs of students

and the actual central administrative functions of student personnel workers has been widened by the increasing centralization of the institutional bureaucracy in higher education. The students are cynical, the faculty contemptuous and other administrators suspicious of the value of these people who fit no clear-cut roles on campus. Students see them as merely parroting and explaining higher administrative decisions while faculty are puzzled by this alien structure which seems to be responsive to no campus constituency. The fact that the dean of students and subdean posts are already being abandoned on some campuses and that at other schools the deans have been left in limbo with most of their policy-making functions removed is clear warning that, questions of professional status aside, student personnel is in deep trouble.

Student personnel is in need of counseling to assist it in setting up some meaningful and understandable goals. For this it might well turn to one of its specialty areas, professional counseling. Since college counseling is also going through a period of self-examination and a reevaluation of its activities, one might reasonably conclude that this would be an exercise in futility, the blind leading the blind. However, there is one fundamental difference in the situations of the two groups: counselors have rarely been challenged about their primary concern for the constituency which they serve (the students) or their academic respectability, while these are the two core areas in which student personnel workers tend to be most suspect in the academic community. The professional counselors are simply expanding on a basic service role through a reordering of priorities in order to increase their effectiveness within the total campus community. Student personnel, on the other hand, with the loss of its disciplinary functions, its direction of student organizations and other parental roles is being forced to search for a rationale for its very existence.

To fill the gap, some student personnel literature, such as the book edited by Siegel (1968), is attempting to revive the Williamson myth of every personnel position as a counseling position, but this strategy is doomed to failure as it neglects to take into consideration that, under present circumstances, student personnel is oriented toward the central administration of the institution whereas counselors, to be effective in helping students work through their problems, must maintain the welfare of their clients as their central and ultimate concern. There can be no ambiguity on this point. Another proposal by a student personnel educator (Silverman, 1971) suggests a negotiator-conciliator role for student personnel workers, but this model seems highly idealistic, for it is difficult to comprehend any group of employees being supported by an organization whose sole purpose is to mediate between contending groups or individuals within the organization. As Silverman points out, this would require that the student personnel worker be in, but not part of, the institution, completely rejecting any of the usual institutional rewards and relying instead for whatever satisfaction he might get from some sort of abstract "professional norms." Assuming that student personnel workers are not devoid of normal human needs for belonging, affiliation and acceptance, this proposal seems highly unrealistic.

It seems more likely that whatever student personnel is to become will have to build on or grow out of the current situation. With the fluidity of events within higher education, those who identify themselves with the status quo or appear to increase the structural chain-of-command rigidities of the system lose their effectiveness with the students. Student personnel, in the eyes of most students, is already bankrupt in this respect—along with student government which deans of students have tended to support and guide and the fraternal system which deans of men and women have devoted countless hours to perpetuate. Little in the practice of student personnel offers a vision of what the future could be if a radical change should occur within the value structure of those who administer student personnel programs. What gains to the students and higher education might accrue if those currently in student personnel positions abandoned their managerial roles in relation to student affairs and adopted roles growing out of the needs and goals of students. The central role of facilitator for students, the bridge between students and the adult power blocs of faculty and administration, seems consistent with the purposes of student personnel as laid out in the training programs for student personnel workers.

Counseling and Student Personnel

Professional counselors have always had the needs of students as their major concern, but their position in the administrative hierarchy has not permitted them, and they have not asked for, the authority to implement changes in the institution which might improve the mental health conditions on campus. Student personnel workers occupy positions of influence and have contact with persons at administrative levels where decisions of significance to the campus are made. The potential for the two groups assisting each other during the transition period is unlimited if, and the if is a big one, counselors could curb their defensiveness about their dependency on the whims of student personnel administrators and student personnel would cease its love-hate relationship with counseling by abandoning the myth that counseling is generic to student personnel.

Student personnel is in a critical position to facilitate the transition between the traditional relationships between students and the institution and the new ones which are already being shaped, since its practitioners are perceived to be closest to the sources of student communication and discontent as well as the sources of administrative decision making. Major changes will occur in line with many of the demands of young people despite the reluctance of adult governing groups. Student personnel will either be eliminated as these changes occur or will become a significant instrument for making the changes less damaging and destructive to the participants. Deans of students and their subdeans already hold positions of influence in relation to students, an influence which has often been used to block and delay the legitimate expression of student grievances. Many of those grievances have ended up in a counselor's office, but the professional counselor has not been in a position to implement changes which might alleviate the grievances. He has been able to do little more than listen sympathetically and, without threatening the power structure, inform appropriate persons on campus of possible causes of student discontent.

At this point the conflict of values between counselors and student personnel workers becomes explicit, for the tendency of student personnel workers is to point out why the conditions cannot be changed or modified. As an arm of the central administration, the student personnel staff is programmed to conduct messages down the chain of command, not synthesize information for interpretation up the organization pipeline for action. The students have recognized this, for the obvious result is that in times of crisis, almost a continuing condition these days, they bypass the deans on most important issues and demand to deal directly with the president. Radical, minority, and dissident students uniformly ignore the entire student personnel apparatus. Even the student government leaders are spending more time in dialogue with the president than with the dean of students. Hodgkinson's survey of presidents' attitudes toward deans of students confirms these opinions (1970).

In increasing numbers, presidents seem to be coming to the conclusion that their student personnel deans are unable to give them assistance in working with important student problems. Even more distressing, the student personnel deans may be ignored as a valuable source of simple information about students and their concerns. Since they communicate with students within the protective confines of their offices or at formal committee meetings, their perceptions of the campus are often restricted and distorted. The result has been the deans are relegated to such ceremonial functions as attending teas and Mom's Club meetings, sitting in on campus-planning committee meetings to give the appearance that student interests are being represented, and organizing public relations activities. Their one administrative responsibility is that of manager and budget officer for the various technical and specialist areas where student contacts occur: the union, financial aids office, student health service, and counseling center. The more time and energy they invest in internal organizational matters, however, the greater is their alienation from students, thus reducing even more their contacts with the constituency which gives student personnel its professional validity.

If the trend continues, there will be little need for student personnel workers to be drawn from the ranks of education. Those who can manage a business office will do just as well and, perhaps, better because their training and experience will have been specifically in business administration. This certainly clarifies the role of the student personnel administrative offices. Without the current pretense that a knowledge of adolescents and counseling is the prerequisite to carrying out the duties of a dean, the managerial-business aspects of the job come into clear focus. The status of the student personnel deans ceases to be built on the shaky foundation of academic affiliation and is drawn entirely from the central administration for their managerial abilities, just as that of the institutional business manager. Since the post of manager of student personnel resources no longer commands a professorship without regard to the usual academic requirements, the faculty can relax their hostility toward what they perceive as an academic charade. Students can be more certain that decisions affecting them are made on the basis of managerial expertise and economic demands rather than on the basis of expediency sugar-coated with educational and philosophical terminology to rationalize their manipulation. And the directors of the specialty areas will find themselves less on the defensive over professional matters; the deans can be expeditors of the work of their specialists, as suggested by Townsend (1970), rather than competitors in setting goals and policies.

While studying adolescent psychology, human development, educational philosophy, and other courses in a program planned to sensitize him to the needs and concerns of college-age students, the student personnel worker seems to be preparing for a career whose central focus will be service to students; whereas, on his job, the client becomes the administration of the institution which hires him. His success is not judged by his effectiveness in promoting student development so much as it is by his ability to protect the central administration from the problems associated with keeping thousands of older adolescents and young adults under control. To achieve this cooling effect, he has had to preside over activities which many of the campus adults considered to be sideshows to the main educational functions of the institution. As pointed out by the sociologist Bisno (1960), when the training of the professional has little relationship to meeting the needs of the clientele for which the professional is allegedly being prepared to serve, it may be counterproductive to the welfare of society. One result may be that the rewards of status expected by the profession are diminished or withheld.

New Myths and Old Realities

Student personnel has drawn on two sources for confirmation of its professional status: the faculty academic ranking system, and the administrative hierarchy. Strangely, student personnel has made no effort to seek status or other rewards from students, the clientele it is ostensibly trained to serve. I know of a case where a popular and effective dean of students is considered "unprofessional" by student personnel workers in other schools because he is on an informal first-name basis with students and views his job as that of a modified ombudsman. Perhaps student personnel, in its attempt to confirm its status with the adult power blocs on campus, has maneuvered itself into a blind alley. The academic rank of most of its practitioners is considered phony by faculty and certainly carries no status in the academic community. Moreover, the designated position title of dean within the administrative hierarchy diminishes their potential effectiveness in working with students. The authority of the dean of students within the central administration is also minimal since his contacts with students are restricted almost exclusively to the straight establishment group and, hence, he has little negotiating communication with those groups who are most likely to force issues to a confrontation with the administration. At the same time, the role of deans in student committees and student government meetings is being viewed with increasing suspicion by the establishment students who are beginning to recognize that this monitoring of their activities can result as much in administrative manipulation as in facilitating their deliberations. For one reason or another, student personnel deans are suspect among each of the other identifiable groups on campus.

Student personnel in its present form is up against the wall. In some institutions, the student personnel structure is being dismantled with deans reassigned to housekeeping activities or summarily dismissed. The tragedy for the profession is that, where these actions are taking place, there has been no word of protest from faculty, or more importantly from students. The so-called Personnel Point of View has done little to convince students that deans are very much concerned about their interests. Rather than leading the reorganization of relationships of higher education to students, stu-

102

dent personnel may become one of its first victims. Nothing less than a complete restructuring of its values and a reordering of its priorities by student personnel can revive the possibility that a profession exists.

If the student personnel deans' offices are converted into managerial offices, using the model of the business manager's position, the results would simply make explicit what many assume already exists. The gap between the ideal of the student-centered functions which are the focus of the professional education of those preparing for student personnel positions and the managerial functions which are actually performed by deans and subdeans has widened to the point where few people on campus take seriously the contention of deans that their first priority is the welfare of students. The managerial model would, however, require student personnel workers to give up any pretensions to being part of a unique professional group. But, more importantly, the adoption of this model will be a serious loss to students. There is within student personnel the potential for providing leadership for the types of learning and human interactions being demanded by students as part of their education. Student personnel has had the potential from its beginning to make a valuable contribution to student welfare but it has become untracked from the goals for which it was originally conceived as a profession.

A true profession must, among other things, have a service orientation, some purpose growing out of the needs of a clientele. While the training of student personnel practitioners is consistent with the preparation of professionals to serve the needs of college students, the primary activities in which those in the student personnel structure have become increasingly engaged, with the exception of those of the professional counselors and health service physicians, are management and central administration oriented. The idealistic phrases about nonclassroom learning and the facilitation of adolescent development become translated into master schedule calendars, the monitoring of student committees, the installation of TV sets and computer outlets in the residence halls and the like. "What have you contributed to the growth or development of students this past week?" Most deans would be hard put to answer this question and, therefore, the legitimacy of the profession is in doubt.

Students have not had the power in the past to assign status, or to give or withhold rewards from the adults in the college community. This is rapidly changing. Student demands for their right to participate in the retention and promotion of the instructional staff are beginning to be heeded. Student representatives are being appointed to faculty and administrative committees. Presidents are including students in their personal advisory boards. And trustees and legislative committees are listening with respect to student witnesses on the conduct of the colleges.

It now appears inevitable that students will become a power to be reckoned with in the college community. Their strength is already apparent in their forcing major modifications of housing rules and regulations as they have abandoned the residence halls in droves and, thus, stimulated a complete reevaluation of the tight-fisted, and often high-handed, adult rule of the student ghettos in which they have previously been required to live. Their gaining control of incidental fee distribution on a number of campuses forecasts serious inroads into areas formerly presided over by student personnel workers. Whoever controls the money available for programming will obviously control the personnel who are permitted to influence that programming. It seems a logical step, therefore, to the position where students will demand a significant role in the selection and retention of those who are to offer them special services. They are already using student fees to hire their own legal counsel, their own tutorial services, and their own leadership training consultants. Why should they not play a significant role in the hiring and retention of their counselors, their activities director, their housing coordinator— and their deans?

There seems to be little question that each year will see a greater impact by students on the status and reward system of the adults in the campus community. This can be an added threat or a positive alternative for student personnel workers. In either case, they will be forced to look more to students for the assignment of their value to the college community. If student personnel workers are required to earn their campus status as much from students as from their meaningless academic rank and the managerial post assigned them by the central administration, they will be forced to make their training preparation functional in their jobs. In other words, with students a part of the grantor system for assigning status and rewards, the emphasis of the profession is placed on the ability of the individual professionals to facilitate ways to meet the needs of the students. Staff members, rather than being primarily concerned with managerial housekeeping tasks, are forced to devote more of their energies to developing the rationale for activities with students. They are required to defend their actions to their constituents—the students. The entire student personnel structure becomes service rather than control oriented and student personnel workers can get down to the job of extra classroom education which they have deluded themselves they have been doing all along.

Professional counselors can play a role in this shift of emphasis, for they are likely to have the skills as well as the orientation necessary for assisting the student personnel staff in its staff development. Counselors have a professional orientation to their job and students which can be helpful to their student personnel colleagues: a purpose growing out of the needs of a clientele. Counselors devote many hours of their staff meeting time to staff development through analyzing their contacts with clients and the rationale for their procedures. They are introspective and self-critical. Introspection and self-evaluation tend to be minimal in the daily press of student personnel work, but they are essential for maintaining professional integrity. Business and industry have recognized the importance of staff development in increasing the effectiveness of their administrative personnel. Strangely, in some college student personnel groups, where one would expect creative approaches to self-development, there is evidence of outright hostility toward the methods currently used in business and industry to facilitate change and open lines of communication. Deans and directors in higher education have, on the other hand, been generally resistant to any form of in-service training or staff development except the superficial "reading the dean's mail" sessions which have become a cliché for student personnel staffs.

The orientation toward its work which student personnel can borrow from its professional counseling colleagues is continuing effort to justify its service activities on some theoretical basis. I do not agree with Penney's contention that student personnel cannot be considered a profession because it lacks the requirement of a unique body of knowledge of its own, that it borrows wholesale from the social sciences, thus confusing the generalist-specialist problem (1968). At present, the issue is not what or how much is borrowed but rather that few of the potential contributions of the other fields which Penney mentions (vocational development, subcultures on campus, human development, and learning) seem to have any significant impact on professional practice. Where are the deans of students who are in a leadership role interpreting vocational development problems of young people to faculty to bring about curriculum revision? Where are those deans who make their case to students regarding student activities on the basis of learning principles? —or even use learning and development principles to guide their own decisions? What deans are making significant contributions to discussions of the problems facing higher education as they relate to young people?

To answer my questions, I believe that in not operating on a set of theoretical principles or on an accumulation of basic knowledge in their daily work activities, student personnel workers are defensive about what they know. This defensiveness prevents them from speaking out as experts, even though it would seem to others that they should be among the most knowledgeable persons on campus in matters where students are concerned. In almost two decades of association with higher education, I can recall very few definitive statements on student affairs made by student personnel workers reported in the local press or released for publication through campus or general publications. Even when publication mechanisms are regularly available, such as a weekly newspaper column devoted to the opinions of the college personnel on any topic or a campus publication created for the same purpose, the student personnel staff has not taken advantage of the opportunity to discuss student concerns or student activities within the context of their expertise. It may be that student personnel workers feel that such publication would reduce their options in a particular campus situation or would embroil their offices in controversy. If this is the case, the loss far outweighs the gain, for leadership and authority cannot be developed in a vacuum of ideas, and the silence of those who are seen as responsible for the quality of the daily lives of thousands of young people gives the strong impression to their student constituencies and their faculty colleagues that they have no ideas or convictions based on theory or drawn from a body of knowledge.

The consequences of this lack of a public stance or a professional orientation can have a very serious effect on the relations between student personnel workers and those with whom they are involved—students, faculty, and the professionals in the specialty service areas. They are psychologically distanced from these people and are regarded with suspicion and then hostility. This is similar to the reactions expressed toward the nationally publicized student in the black bag who appeared in a college classroom a few years ago. The other students totally ignored this living object who sat in on the class but did not speak. Then the other students began to question what right "it" had to be in their class and, finally, there was an outpouring of anger toward this uncommunicative object which would not reveal its purposes for being present. Interestingly, the professor who used this technique in an attempt to impress on his students the reactions of people toward things they do not understand was himself the object of considerable hostility by others on campus and around the state for his unexplained use of the classroom in this manner. There is little doubt that we need to know where we stand with others in relation to their goals. We fill our uncertainties with suspicion and, then, anger. The student personnel worker is the man in the black bag for the rest of the campus. Few know where he really stands on issues and so they suspect that he acts capriciously or arbitrarily.

For faculty, feelings for the campus black bag man do not ordinarily go beyond the point of ignoring or mild suspicion about

107

his intentions. He does not threaten them for he seems to be more engaged with the kids' games than with the central issues which affect the real purposes of the college as the faculty perceive them. For the specialist, such as the professional counselor, the uncertainties about what their student personnel colleagues believe about the relationship of students to the campus community and its meaning for their specialized services can be disconcerting and demoralizing. The counselor, for instance, fills his uncertainties with suspicions that he is an affront to deans who see themselves as counselors, because he is a continuing reminder to the deans of the gap which exists between their counselor identity and their actual job practices. He is also suspicious that deans may resent his freedom to operate within the student-centered value system which student personnel has claimed as its primary motivating force. For the students, the ambiguity of student personnel is translated into making deans the symbol of the arbitrary authority of the institution. On few campuses can a dean arbitrarily dismiss or punish a student behind his (or her) closed office door, but this reality of the past remains as a legacy of suspicion and hostility among students. In the upheaval in higher education in which arbitrary authority is being replaced by cooperative arrangements or arbitration procedures between equals, the students are gaining a significant role as one of the participants. So long as those in student personnel remain silent about this trend and appear to give ground only when under pressure, they will lose the opportunity to earn the respect from students they will need in order to work effectively with them under the new conditions.

However, those in student personnel will not be able to create a new image among students simply by talking about their concerns for students. They will have to validate their new orientation by their actions and responses to student needs. The opportunities for revamping the profession are tremendous, for the groundwork is already laid, but student personnel workers will need to learn new methods of operation tied in more closely with explicit theoretical concepts to replace the unworkable arbitrary authority model which makes their position on campus an anachronism. One possible model is that of student learning facilitator. The students themselves have been calling attention to the fact that they do not arrive at college as disembodied intellects to be stacked away in little cells, fed a diet of knowledge units in the classroom, and manipulated as social security numbers. They are telling us in every way possible that they are emotional human beings with a variety of previous experiences facing one of the most critical developmental periods of their lives.

They need to learn much more than the classroom can offer about themselves and the environment in which they live. They are asking for assistance in investigating areas of greater immediate consequence to themselves than their formal classroom requirements can cover. And they are asking for opportunities to experience warm, close relationships with other people in which they can learn how to look at themselves and what impact they have on others. The result has been student-organized experimental colleges, student-initiated sensitivity and confrontation groups, and student-operated volunteer activities in the community. With few of these has the student personnel staff been involved. And yet, these are the types of activities with which they should and must be engaged if they are truly concerned about extracurricular (or cocurricular) learning as they profess to be. Students are engaged in a search for self-definition and self-fulfillment, and their activities, rather than being merely amusements or time fillers, are the vehicle for finding themselves. This may be one reason that the traditional institutionalized student activities which student personnel workers have monitored over the years are reaching only a fraction of the student body. Most students are not satisfied with merely earning Brownie Points from their living groups for serving on dance committees, nit picking over decorations for a faculty tea, or arguing about the fine points of Robert's Rules of Order at a student government meeting. These pointless tasks are being left to the untroubled middle segment of the student body, the group with which student personnel administrators have been most comfortable. As the range of student types has increased, the student personnel worker has lost his effectiveness because of his inability to cut these new student types to fit the old patterns.

The establishment of separate minority affairs offices, experi-

109

mental colleges, volunteer organizations, and other special interest groups outside the student personnel structure should be a clear indication that students do not feel that that structure can cope with or be of any direct assistance in activities involving the different, odd, or creative students. The fact that adolescent development and the psychology of individual differences are core courses in the training programs for the various deans on the staff seems to make little or no difference. Deans continue to talk in terms of methods of control and restraint, and many are amused at the efforts of students to "get organized."

It is the rare dean who will talk in learning or developmental theory terms at any level. Discussions of new residence halls are likely to center on cost per square foot rather than the needs of older adolescents as they relate to such matters as grouping, privacy, and coed activities. It has not been the leadership of student personnel that has brought the acceptance of coed living but the students' voting for this form of living arrangement by moving out of residence halls into private housing where they can make their own rules and regulations. Coed living and modifications of residence halls regulations is due to the simple economic fact that those halls must now compete on the open market to attract the students to pay for their building and maintenance costs.

It is interesting (or is it tragic?) that as students have acquired greater power to bring economic pressure to bear on some areas, the moral justification of the student personnel people administering these areas for maintaining the status quo has tended to disappear; this confirms for students that student personnel workers have operated from a framework of political and economic expediency, not from any basic concern for students or from any theoretical or academic rationale. In like manner, the new student sees the deans' offices as closely identified with the fraternity-sorority system as a means of subsidizing the system. He recognizes that through the support of deans of men and women, the system has relieved colleges of substantial building costs and served as a conservative stabilizing force within the student body. While the deans have rationalized their support of these bastions of the status quo and matchmaking centers for the upward mobile WASPS on the basis that some students learned leadership skills and others learned good grooming and table manners, virtually everyone on campus shared the open secret that the tit-for-tat agreement between the central administration and the fraternal system was to support each other in maintaining the status quo. Even though deans should have been able to recognize from their course work in psychology that forcing young adolescents to choose the one group of people to whom they would be bound through four years of their development after only a few days of intense excitement and anxiety doesn't make common or psychological sense, they have raised few questions about the system on theoretical grounds, giving in to modifications of the rush procedure only when the faculty or registrar complained about interference with registration or when the idle hours of the brothers and sisters between their arrival for rush and their first day of classes began to result in off-campus complaints of antisocial behavior. A specialist in management, with no background in psychology, adolescent development, or any training in the handling of young people could have made decisions about the student body in ways which they have been made by student personnel administrators, and with much less cynicism generated within the student body.

If student personnel is to become a profession, decisions must be made from a body of knowledge related to the clientele being served. Student personnel has long paid lip service to the concept that important student learning goes on outside the formal classroom. The concept is a sound one and, as I have said, is central to the student protest about their college education. The fact that students are now making this point themselves without reference to the student personnel point of view is instructive. It seems reasonable to ask why student personnel workers have not been a greater force in pressing this attitude toward learning on the college campus. The battle now rages between students and faculty with student personnel remaining remarkably neutral. Again, a leadership role has been abandoned, perhaps because the student personnel

111

workers find themselves unwilling to alienate faculty through supporting a student cause. They are much more comfortable in the role of explaining to students what the limits of their powers are. They are unskilled in the methods of assisting students in achieving their goals or meeting their needs. They are also uncertain about the types of students who are active in trying to bring about changes within the institution since their contacts are primarily with those middle-of-the-road "establishment" students who furnish the recruits for the usual student activities programs.

Student personnel must turn itself around. The president may want to have on his staff one person who handles the business details of the various student personnel offices, but those in contact with students must view their roles as growing out of the needs of the students, not out of the administrative requirements of the institutional bureaucracy. Currently, student personnel is viewed as an appendage of the real work of higher education. As a professional, the student personnel worker must view his activities as inseparable from the concerns of students and others who interact with young people. The roles assigned to student personnel are becoming decreasingly essential for the welfare and development of the students. Students are indicating in numerous ways that they can survive quite adequately without the type of attention traditionally paid to them by student personnel workers. If the student personnel worker sees his task as contributing to the overall process of adolescent development, then a new meaning can be given to his work. It seems obvious that he would, then, have to begin drawing on the knowledge he has accumulated from his academic work during his training period.

As students assume more of the housekeeping tasks for themselves and eliminate most of the rules and regulations whose enforcement has consumed most of the time of student personnel workers, the profession must develop a purpose of significance to the institution it serves. That is not a very difficult task considering that the training programs have been preparing professionals toward playing just such a significant role on campus. The current state of decline for student personnel has resulted from the fact that, once trained,

112

the degreed graduate has moved into a position in which he has used his training and knowledge very little, if at all, shifting from student needs and concerns to central administration control functions. The time has come for practice and preparation to become consistent; then, a true profession will emerge.

Center for
Human Resources

EIGHT

In tracing the history of the college counseling center and examining its service rationale, not only are the sources of its present problems evident but also the sources of its potential for making significant contributions to the total campus community. From its beginnings the central concern of the center has been to make the college experience more meaningful and rewarding for the students who come for assistance. With their guidance orientation, the centers growing out of the Veterans' Administration Bureaus of World War II offered educational and vocational advice to assist students choose appropriate college and career goals. It became evident,

114

however, that no matter how technically skillful the counselor was in using the basic tools of testing and occupational information, students were frequently left with many important questions about themselves unanswered.

Stimulated by the writing of Rogers (1942, 1951), counselors came to recognize success with clients was dependent on the counselor's ability to convey concern for the client as a person. As the central technique for improving the client's situation, the relationship itself was accepted as the focus of professional counseling. And basic to the relationship were the counselor's communications skills: active listening, and synthesizing responses. The ability to communicate effectively is the asset which counselors bring to their positions; however, the need for them to develop a personal relationship with individuals in order to do a significant job is being questioned by those who pay the bills. This latter source of difficulty for the role of the professional counselor has been discussed at length previously. The emphasis in this chapter is on the areas in which a counseling center can make significant contributions to the campus. The communication skills which the staff possess will continue to be important, but they will have to be used in different ways than through individual counseling if they are to stand up under a cost-analysis evaluation.

Some personal counseling with students by professional staff will continue—but with an expanded purpose. The goal will not only be the growth and development of the individual client, although that will continue to be important, but rather a source of input to the center for insights into the functioning of parts of the campus community. The counselor will not only ask himself: "What can I do to help this student to cope most effectively with his situation?" but also "What is this student telling me about his situation which raises questions (or confirms what I have already learned) about some aspect of the campus which is resulting in problems for students?" The individual counseling becomes, in this system, one form of research on student attitudes and concerns to be used with (or followed by) other methods of data collection for evaluating the functioning of parts of the campus community. Obviously, the counselors will not break the confidences of individual clients or pass judgment about the impact of some segment of the institution on the complaint of one or two clients. But their contacts with the students who are facing difficulties in decision making or coping with institutional pressures will serve as an "early warning" device for initiating more extensive investigations of what appear to be general sources of friction between the student and the institution.

Eliminating or reducing the friction between students and the institution, however, should not be the only motivation for the counselor's listening perceptively to what students are saying about their condition. The college and university structure has a long tradition. It is unlikely that within the foreseeable future the compartmentalized departments and schools will disappear; chairmen and institutional staff are human and very few are willing to abandon the identifications which affirm their status and position. Only a small fraction of the academics are prepared to accept the importance of student learning outside the formal classroom as a fundamental need of students in their personal development. Confronting the professor or the academic administrator with the inadequacies of the present system for the healthy development of college-age students appears, at this point, to be futile—and certainly presumptuous for a counseling center staff.

It would appear that the old cliché "If you can't beat 'em, join 'em" holds the greatest promise for broadening the possibilities for students to grow and develop as human beings. The counseling center can take a leadership position in creating new ways for students to achieve personal satisfaction—working with students and sympathetic faculty to invent meaningful experiences for students in those areas of student need which have come to the attention of counselors.

The center must be active in focusing attention on the needs of college students and methods of meeting those needs within the institution. At a simple level this may mean the staff's assisting in the creation of so-called experimental colleges. It may mean the training of upperclassmen and graduate students to conduct groups within schools or departments in which students can learn more about themselves and the meaning of their goals within those academic areas. It may mean the collection of information about student concerns and attitudes which can be fed into the academic structure for humanizing the procedures used by the faculty and administration. And it may mean the invention and implementation of mechanisms for improving the interactions between faculty and students and students and administrators to resolve the potential conflicts.

Unless the counseling center staff moves into the roles of "early warning" system for reducing campus friction and facilitator for procedures to increase the full human development of students, these roles will have to be invented by the institution. The institutions of higher education are caught in a major conflict between the necessities of the time and the values demands of their students. They have been growing at a phenomenal rate—even so-called small colleges have been growing at high percentage rates so that they face the same crowded classroom, multiple section and student-teacher ratio problems of the larger schools, although on a smaller scale.

One result of the student explosion has been the inability of the institution to deal with students in personalized ways that have been used in the past. Student choices have been sharply curtailed by machine processes which distribute them evenly among sections and close them out of preferred (or even required) courses. Even with the best of planning, classrooms are jammed, and some students may have to sit in hallways. Professors who formerly used discussion methods for teaching and essay exams for evaluation have been forced to lectures and multiple-choice tests. Student contacts with advisors have been reduced to the minimum. Relationships with the institution which had previously been carried on through informal agreements within a general academic code have now been rigidified through legally binding contracts and procedures. Students are in the paradoxical position of having gained almost complete freedom in the areas of dress, speech, and residence requirements

117

while, at the same time, losing considerable freedom to choose in some matters related to their academic programs: professors, class time, preferred elective courses, and so on.

While the areas normally controlled by the student personnel staff have been increasingly released from administrative restrictions due in part to the impossibility of enforcing regulations, students feel themselves more severely manipulated by the system in the academic area. The withdrawal of direct adult supervision in the student personnel area, coupled with the increased mechanical control of students in the academic area, has had the net effect of eliminating almost all significant contact between students and the professional adults on campus.

This reduction in the amount and quality of contact between students and the professional adults has come precisely at a time when the students themselves are demanding that their education be meaningful, that it contribute to their development as human beings. The students entering college are by and large more sophisticated, more physically mature, more idealistic and more concerned about values than any previous college generation. By the sheer numbers in which they have arrived at institutions of higher education, however, they have become the victims of a condition in which alienation might be expected to be a natural component. Loneliness and lack of personal commitment for the ordinary student are virtually built into the normal operating procedures; for, as a person, he rarely makes contact with those adults who comprise the functioning core of the institution. If he lives in the hotel-like dormitory, he probably reacts like the isolated city dweller who protects himself behind a psychological shell from all but a few of those with whom he comes in contact. If he lives in a town apartment, his contacts with the campus may be restricted to class attendance and library work. If he is married, he is not part of the town and the institution is not geared to his needs. The student's chance for meaning in an institutional setting which is struggling to cope in minimal ways with the flood of young people is unlikely to be answered satisfactorily unless some part of the institution takes the initiative to create opportunities for humanizing the educational experience. Students, having gained almost absolute freedom in regard to their personal lives while they are attending college, are turning their energies to the inadequacies which they perceive in the academic area. Their first assault is against the most obvious alienating factor in their academic experience—the teaching process. What the students are saying very loudly is: "You don't care about us!" and most instructors don't (or can't). In fact, most instructors are unaware that caring about the learner makes a difference in the learning.

The counseling center would have a full-time activity if it devoted its energies completely to the investigation of and the communication to the campus community about the process of higher education, student development, and the learning and motivation of young adults. The counseling center must become a center for the conservation and development of the human potential which is represented by the thousands of students who populate its particular campus. The center must be the generator of improved interactions between the various groups on campus but, most important, between instructional staff and students.

With their training pointed inwardly toward the counseling or clinical process, the center staff lose sight of the purpose that their work activity has as related to the educational process of the institution. They have tended to view their contacts with students as a replacement for the interactions which students were not having with the other adults on campus. The center has lost its orientation to the total academic process of the institution. Center staffs have become so encapsulated in a therapy-for-its-own-sake orientation that they are often immobilized when asked to account for what they are doing or to justify their activities. How, after all, does one justify one's activities as a replacement for someone else's responsibilities —particularly if the replacement is more costly than the original? The answer, of course, is that it can't be done and as this is being written, counseling centers involved primarily in psychotherapy at two major colleges have recently been elminated, attesting to the fact that the logic of free psychotherapy for those lucky enough to be enrolled at college is being challenged as budgets tighten.

The counseling center must become an integral part of the

119

educational process of the institution. As Danskin (1969) puts it: "the personal involvement of the teacher himself cannot be replaced. Rather, it seems crucial to find ways of strengthening and extending his commitment to the human concerns of education. In a Mc-Luhanesque society which appears schizophrenically fluid to youth forced against their will into cynically dismissing the structure of their elders' world, the college teacher must become meaningfully available to students." I agree with Danskin's conclusion that "the business of the college counselor is to assist the classroom teacher to find ways and resources for focusing upon the human concerns of his students," as well as with his observation that counseling centers which specialize in caring about the individual concerns of students can have the effect of relieving classroom teachers from the feelings of guilt about not devoting time to the human concerns of students.

In a perverse way, the operation of traditional counseling centers may have had the effect of blocking the types of radical changes which are needed in higher education to make the educational enterprise as a whole a more humane experience for students. Although it may sound strange, the counseling center must turn itself into a human resources center for the welfare of the institution as a whole. The attitudes of the staff of the human resources center will differ radically from those of current counseling center staff. Interest and concern will be concentrated on methods by which the center can humanize the educational experiences of students through existing agents rather than on better or more efficient ways of injecting special humanizing experiences into a decreasingly human environment.

A few counseling centers have recently begun to move in the direction I am proposing, but there are as yet no established models where the process has been completed. In some cases, the centers have moved staffs onto the campus in a variety of roles and, in others, the centers have been collapsed into the general personnel services area with titles such as: student development center. The model I am proposing is, however, dependent more upon the attitudes which the staff take toward their services than upon the organizational structure or even the specific activities in which the staff members engage. As long as the staff view themselves as offering adequate services which replace functions not maintained by other campus personnel or as injecting an additional service into the ongoing educational process to make up for a function the staff feel is not being offered by other campus personnel, the center will still be philosophically a traditional center. In very simple terms, the traditional center offers services to the campus community, and its own personnel carry out those services; if the staff withdraw from offering that service, the activity stops. The human resources center will work with and through the people and structure of the campus. When a specific job is completed, its effects will hopefully have left a permanent change, and there will be people indigenous to the situation who will be able to continue critical facets of the activity initiated by the human resources center personnel.

One example of this type of involvement points up the possibilities in the center's working directly with instructional staff. In this case, the center staff were invited by some of the law school faculty to collaborate in a course dealing with psychology and the law. The faculty had recognized that their curriculum, with its emphasis on legal issues, theory, reading cases and the like, tended to leave the students with little feeling for or sensitivity to the fact that they would, as lawyers, be dealing with people. The curriculum gave few opportunities for the students to learn interviewing skills, questioning witnesses, courtroom behavior, and other interpersonal behavior. With the assistance of the center, a program was developed involving law students (and their wives) in the exploration of human relations issues through a confrontation group format using interpersonal exercises. The reaction of all those involved was enthusiastic, including the wives who are an important part of the stress situation for married students. Student reports indicated that they felt they became more comfortable and more effective in a client interviewing practicum which they were taking concurrently with the human relations program. The question as to whether the program has made a permanent impact on the law school will have to wait until it is determined whether the law school faculty and senior students are able to continue the program themselves with minimal assistance from the center's staff.

Another example of input into the academic area is a project carried out by a center with a department of architecture. Here, again, the center staff worked directly within a catalog course, assisting the instructor to provide a humanistic course dealing with psychological and human factors, not only through the usual readings and lectures but through direct group experiences. Emphasis was placed on the illogical and irrational responses of people so that the prospective architects would incorporate these dimensions of human behavior in their frame of reference. The hope has been that the future architect would be more effective in communicating with his clients as well as being more sensitive to the needs of his clients in his design work. Again, if the burden of carrying out the project remains with the center staff, the impact on the department of architecture may be minimal; but if the instructor was involved in a way which would enable him to carry on the project with little direct assistance from the center, the effect on the department could be significant.

In still another case, the instructors in a great books seminar were assisted by a center's staff to develop ways of recreating the experiences of the authors and characters in books the students were reading through psychodrama and role playing. By acting out situations and ideas represented in the printed words of the authors, the students were able to translate the written word into a visual and feeling medium. This action orientation had the effect of humanizing the classroom for the students and also turned the historical material into current conflicts and problems with which the students could identify more readily; thus, two of the criticisms of the typical formal course were met.

Contributions of the human resources center to the improvement of instruction need not be limited to individual courses and programs. One complaint of students (more often than not justified) is that they cannot reach their professors. To defend the professors on the basis that few students come to talk with them during their posted office hours is to miss the point of the complaint. It is not merely that the professor is not available in his office but also that faculty-student contacts both in and out of classes are characterized by psychological distance: the professor and student play their roles which require the student to be appropriately deferent and awed and the professor to be appropriately aloof and paternal.

For many, the ability to have meaningful interactions goes beyond the so-called generation gap to a lack of skill; the professor and student often do not know how to go about establishing a meaningful dialogue. To help faculty perceive students as human and to help students to be more open and responsive with professors, centers have conducted communications workshops which bring the two groups together to work on problems in interactions. At the request of a group of engineering students, one center staff devoted a full day to teaching a group of engineering students and faculty methods of opening up communications. One follow-up result was the remodeling of one of his courses by a participant faculty member to allow for maximum student participation—an almost unheard of move in this very technically oriented school. Another result was a student-faculty committee (including one of the center staff) which researched faculty advising procedures and, then, published its results to general campus acclaim.

To be maximally effective, the center must be sensitive to potential spin-off results of its work and move quickly to encourage those which give promise of involving participants in the original effort in other humanizing and communication-improving activities. This is particularly true in work with specific groups (such as the faculty of a department or a group of students with a particular concern), for the center staff could easily find itself tied down to a never-ending list of requests to lead groups and, hence, would simply be substituting group work for its current individual counseling. Those students, faculty or administration requests for group leadership assistance should be screened as to their potential for the wider implication of time investment.

If, for instance, a group of student leaders request a leadership training course, the center staff might comply if the leaders agreed to share their experiences and new understandings with the committees and organizations with which they work. The one-shot talk on leadership or the short encapsulated series of meetings, with no plan for follow-up, should be rejected. Too often counseling staff have become involved in this type of activity which makes the participants feel good ("I've taken a course in group leadership!") but has almost no effect on the general activities of the institution or even the organizations of which the participants are leaders.

Centers frequently receive requests from residence halls for involvement in a variety of activities. Because they contain high concentrations of students in generally controllable circumstances, residence halls make an excellent contact point for center staff; however, too many of the activities have been public relations jobs for the center or unproductive short contact sessions with little follow-up value. There has been a move to establish branch offices in residence halls, but here, too, the center staff member can become bogged down picking up individual cases. The staff member, if he is to be of more than immediate value to a few individual students, must view his location in the residence unit as an opportunity to improve the general psychological climate in the unit so that the experiences of the majority of the students in that unit will be improved. All too often, the student's experience in the living unit, particularly the traditional dormitory, is merely a further intensification of the depersonalization and alienation that he encounters in other phases of his college life.

One center undertook to develop a strategy which would build a more effective human community within a specific living unit housing four hundred men. The unit was divided into sections with each section containing a resident assistant and about twenty-five students. The center staff worked with each assistant and one or two students selected from each section. These people were put through a training program dealing with the social psychology of groups, group dynamics techniques, communication skills, the development of cohesion within groups, and the creation of the feeling of community among the sections. The plan was to emphasize the quality of human community in this living unit and to attempt to integrate this with the broader educational experience of each stu-

124

dent. By developing more meaningful reference groups for each student, it was hoped that he would become involved in his education and able to use his personal resources in learning. By increasing the quality of interactions of the residents their personal development would be enhanced. Early results of the program have been quite promising. A by-product of the program is to give a group of assistants and sixteen undergraduates an opportunity to serve in a helping role for which they have been well prepared over an extended period of time. The program also has the potential of creating a pool of well-qualified student leaders for subsequent freshman orientation groups in a much richer and more meaningful manner. Again, the potential for spin-off from the program in helping those on campus help others makes the program a worthwhile investment for the center staff.

Still another type of program involves the center staff with living units in making their contacts with their elected faculty fellows more useful and productive. Among these efforts is the development by the students and the faculty, with the help of center staff, of a variety of participation formats to increase the contacts between the faculty and students and to decrease the psychological distance between them. The function of the center staff is to help the participants learn how they can interact most effectively, thereby developing a greater sense of community within the institution. Hopefully, the increased ability to communicate between the students and faculty participating will generalize so that those students will be able to approach other faculty members more confidently and the faculty will feel at ease with other students with whom they come in contact.

In each of the above examples, parts of the institution invited center staff in to help them work on a human relations problem, but the personnel of a human resources center cannot wait for invitations for assistance. It must actively engage in efforts to discover what is going on in the institution and to translate its findings into information which is understandable to faculty, students, and administration. The staff member must become what Danskin (1969) calls an educational personnel researcher. The data he collects "must be used to help students and faculty (and administrators) become acutely aware and appreciative of the experiences characterizing the students' daily lives—and how those experiences contribute to or detract from the developmental goals set by the students and faculty."

As Danskin perceptively points out, this function has yet to be invented, for current personnel are not trained to be sensitive to the ongoing experiences of students within the institution which have impact on their lives. Most research is currently of a pre-post test variety rather than aimed at the ongoing life study of students. Little is directed toward specific program analysis, the effects of various educational methods on different types of students. Those who see themselves as educational researchers are primarily interested in the purity of their methods and research design and have little understanding of higher education, learning and motivation, or student development. They are not equipped to ask appropriate questions.

The educational personnel researcher requires a basic orientation toward higher education and a willingness to work with faculty and administrators in a team approach to the educational lives of students. Unless he can involve the faculty and administration in his efforts, his results are likely to end up in a musty file. Those who are affected by the results must be committed to the process by which the results are obtained.

Much needs to be learned regarding the effect of the educational experience on the student. If the center hopes to improve the quality of the student's education and the quality of the human environment of the campus, it needs to have much more specific and reliable information about what is going on in the institution—and especially about the effect of its own activities. If the center is to serve any sort of consultative function on the campus, it can only do so if it is able to account for the effectiveness of its procedures. Every activity in which the center becomes involved needs careful study and evaluation. Otherwise, the staff will find itself tilting at immediately interesting windmills. New programs are adopted and implemented with great enthusiasm by one or two staff members who devote little, if any, time or effort to gathering data on their effectiveness or limitations. The result is that the activity has only a passing impact, often dropped as soon as the particular staff member loses interest or leaves the center. In this period of close scrutiny of all educational activities by budget-conscious administrators, such offhand involvement by center staff could be disastrous to the continuation of the center itself.

As the center moves into new activities, the need for evaluation is all the more important. There is no history of experience to gauge the effectiveness of programs such as those described. New models of evaluation will have to be developed because the impact of the programs is in their design to be preventative and enriching rather than remedial. The simple head counting of cases as in the past is completely inadequate for measuring the effectiveness of the center's efforts. Moreover, since the institutions continue to change rapidly (if only in terms of numbers), the evaluations of programs will have to be made constantly. Functions which once were relevant and valuable may later be considered counterproductive. Ongoing, systematic research is indispensable to the continued effectiveness of every unit of the institution—and especially to a human resources center.

The center staff, as implied earlier, will have the additional responsibility of communicating meaningful information related to the educational enterprise to faculty, administrators, and students designed to encourage them to think about education with respect to the extent and ways students change during a particular part of their experience—a course or a period in a living group, for instance.

This communication would help the campus community focus on the effects of current educational processes. The information, and its presentation, must not arouse defensive reactions from those toward whom it is directed. It is not the job of the center's staff to pass judgments on other parts of the campus community. The information should be directed toward what is happening— what the effects of an experience seem to be. Decisions about the incorporation of this information have to be left up to those who

127

are responsible for the programs or activities investigated. This is one good reason why those whose activities or programs are being investigated should be part of the investigating team.

But equally important to the input of information, the institution desperately needs facilitators of communication between students, faculty and administrators. As Danskin puts it (1969): "Even as industrial personnel workers facilitate joint planning and negotiations between workers and management, or aid on the redefinition of roles resulting from continuous change, so educational personnel workers must become communication facilitators with students, faculty and administrators if orderly change is to occur in higher education." The students are quite obviously asking to share in the decision-making process of the institution. Events on numerous campuses indicate that it is just as obvious that students will gain an increasing voice in the affairs of the institution which directly affect students. The inclusion of students as an influential power bloc by the faculty and administration is inevitable, but the process will take place as part of a cooperative community action resulting in a steady series of rational steps or as the result of irrational confrontations between hostile groups. The institutions of higher education cannot afford the latter. The educational specialist can make a major contribution to the survival of higher education by developing the mechanisms necessary for a community effort at resolution of the problem of incorporating students in the decision-making processes of colleges and universities. Student needs and concerns must be heard and implemented.

Success in integrating students into the campus community, however, will be dependent not only on working out accommodations with faculty and administrators but also on assisting the students to develop meaningful communications among themselves. Student government as presently constituted cannot adequately deal with faculty and administration as the voice of the students. With the student government apparatus designed for the undergraduate population of an earlier paternalistic era, the student representatives elected to student senates do not represent those needs which must be given attention by the power structure on campus if the institution is to avoid continuing turmoil. Graduate students, married students, ethnic minorities, women, commuters, and other special interest groups must have direct access to the communication systems within the student power structure. Because of its lack of viable constituencies, the present structure gives advantage to self-aggrandizement and the politically oriented Greek system and, therefore, is unreliable as a source of feedback about the sentiments of the general student body.

Efforts are being made at some institutions to gain input from groups outside the traditional student political framework through special retreats and workshops to which representatives of obvious minority groups (such as blacks) are being invited. These are a good beginning but are too often seen by the adults as safety valves to allow students with grievances to blow off steam at faculty and administrators rather than as part of the ongoing process of community governance. The nonstudent sector of the institution must guard against the tendency to align itself with those in the self-serving business of simply perpetuating a structure which increasingly alienates itself from the bulk of its potential constituencies. Fundamental rearrangements of student participation in campus governance must be encouraged and supported by the faculty and administration. The human resources center personnel have a critical role to play in creating the communication conditions which will facilitate this change in relations among the students and the other two power blocs on campus.

Another focus of attention for the human resources personnel is the instructional staff. Human interactions of the instructional staff with students cannot be replaced. But it is important that the teachers be assisted in understanding the needs and motivations of students and their own activities as they affect the learning process. In higher education, teaching has been viewed almost exclusively as a modeling process: students are somehow to become enthusiastic about a field of study through an osmotic transaction with an instructor who conveys his enthusiasm for his own research activities to his pupils. This model may have some validity at the graduate level and with certain specific teacher-researchers but there is considerable evidence, not the least of which is the overwhelming consensus of undergraduate students, that the instruction in higher education leaves something to be desired. No one model of the teacher-learner transaction will suffice for all students, all instructors, and all courses, as Rogers' (1969) book has so vividly demonstrated, and as counseling psychologists, with their background in individual differences, should very well know. The personnel of the human resources center can, as an initial step, make opportunities available for instructional staff to share their teaching experiences as well as communicating to them information about the learning process. Unless the product which the student is purchasing in the classroom is improved, the classroom will continue to be a source of stress and strain within the campus community.

In general, the human resources center must give first priority to the areas of tension within the institutions of higher education which threaten to destroy those institutions unless the sources of stress are eliminated. The personnel of the center will need to develop their skills in ways which will permit them to act confidently in bridging the communication barriers which now exist on the typical college campus. Such communications seem crucial to transforming our institutions of higher education into real communities which permit optimum learning.

I have written previously of the inadequacy of the current training of counseling psychologists for the task with which they are faced on the college campus. In this final section, I want to come at this issue from a different angle and to expand on my critique to include the training programs for student personnel generally, for it seems that the staff of the human resources center will need to be increased beyond the traditional counseling types to incorporate many of the personnel who are now employed in the various personnel services areas.

There is without any doubt a discrepancy between existing student services and training programs, and the functions which I am proposing are critically needed in higher education. Current services and training programs, with few exceptions, focus primarily on meeting the mundane student needs for housing, information about financial aids, job interview scheduling, the alleviation of anxiety when faced with a personal problem, and so on. They also exist to meet the institution's need for regulating (or giving the appearance of regulating) the potentially disruptive behavior of students. Service personnel have not seen themselves in roles which facilitate change in their institutions—these roles must be given first priority if the professions involved, as well as the institutions, are to survive.

The professions are faced with a chicken-and-egg dilemma: do the personnel staffs take the initiative to sell a set of new functions to administrators who have hired them for specific housekeeping tasks? Do the training departments revamp their programs to give new graduates skills which have not yet been asked for by the administrations of colleges and universities? Does the profession do a "selling" job within higher education and attempt to create a demand? Obviously, the initial impetus for any change will have to come out of the student services personnel themselves in one way or another. That counseling, as well as the other student services, is under mounting pressure to justify its existence is motivation enough for the specialty groups within the profession of student services to take some bold new steps in redefining their activities. The first step in any remaking of student services will have to be the conviction on the part of those in the field that the old forms and functions must be discarded. Having accepted this premise, the search for new formats should follow naturally both within the established service groups and also within the training program.

This is easier said than done, however, because those in present positions as deans and directors of service operations and directors of training programs have a vested interest in the current situation remaining exactly as it is. And those of us in the student services areas have not been known for our bold approaches to problems or our willingness to take risks and break with convention. Our most daring innovations have generally involved the "tinkering with titles" on tables or organization in which deans of men and women disappear to be replaced by one male associate dean and one female associate dean or in which a counselor is renamed an assistant director for research or training.

Our great need is to generate a ferment of new ideas and totally new attitudes within our professional groups. The fundamental questioning required for a revamping of the profession might begin with the establishment of local, regional, and national conferences which would include personnel service workers from various specialties, students, and college administrators charged with discussing potential new models for the student services areas. The support for these conferences could come from the professional organizations to which the members of our professional specialties belong. These groups also need to develop research and consultant grants to investigate and give leadership to the implementation of student personnel services planning to operate within new service models. The professional organizations themselves would receive a new lease on life if they had some operational purpose for existence beyond their current tendency to engage almost exclusively in professional masturbation.

The professional groups might also support preprofessional internship for outstanding graduate students to work in those few personnel programs which are attempting to apply new models in their work and to carry out research which is relevant to the types of functions which have been described. The professional groups might encourage the establishment of local, regional, and national committees to work on the interdisciplinary problems of research which will be required to make investigations meaningful to higher education.

The professional organizations to which the members of specialties belong should serve as generators for the complete rethinking necessary for revamping student personnel services. But, beyond this, these organizations should create means by which new experimental programs can be established, supported, and researched, much as the federal government has established, supported, and researched experimental ventures in agriculture, forestry, and urban development.

Center for Human Resources

As this is being written, counseling and the other student personnel functions in higher education are in serious trouble. The form which these services will take within the next decade is going to change. The changes will occur either as a reaction to forces generated outside the student services areas or as a result of a bold and creative effort on the part of the service areas to redefine themselves in meaningful ways which contribute to the general welfare of higher education. Student services have no choice about changing. Their only choice is whether these changes will occur through their own efforts or result from the manipulations and directives of others.

Outreach Functions Performed by College Counseling Centers

APPENDIX

The following items are the compilation of responses to Thomas Magoon's 1970 Counseling Center Data Bank question asking the respondent to list all "outreach" activities carried on by the staff in his center. Except for minor editing, the responses appear in the form in which they were received from the 204 centers which replied. The lack of precise definition of terms and statements of quality and quantity of staff involvement in some of the statements is more than offset by the total impact of this list, which could be conveyed in no other way.

The most obvious impression which the reader receives is the wide variety of activities in which counseling center staffs are currently involved beyond their typical counseling work. The second fact which emerges is that only about 10 per cent of the centers do not report some outreach activities. One purpose of reproducing these Data Bank responses is to make available to the reader a range of service possibilities for the college counseling center. Hopefully, this listing will result in experimentation with new services at an increasing number of centers, while, at the same time, impressing the staffs of counselor education programs with the need to reevaluate the adequacy of their preparation of college counselors. Another purpose is to offer concrete evidence in support of a major thesis of this book—that a reversal must occur (and, indeed, seems already to be occurring) from a passive to an active approach of the counseling center staff to its campus constituencies.

My thanks to David H. Mills of the University of Maryland counseling center, who, in Magoon's absence, conducted the 1970 survey and gave permission for the use of the Data Bank information.

1. A. Orientation and in-service training provided for residence hall assistants. Group programs provided on human sexuality, drug use and abuse.
   B. Series of How to Study seminars provided for disadvantaged students.
   C. Also consulting services provided for academic departments and other student services divisions.
2. No reply.
3. A. Training several target groups in some basic interviewing skills, for example, black tutors, students manning the crisis telephone.
4. A. Teaching courses in personal growth for psychology credit.
5. A. Campus chaplain program in dormitories is supervised by psychological services.

135

B. Participate in selection and training of residence hall personnel.

6. A. Workshop programs with residence hall staffs.

   B. Consulting with different colleges in areas of student curriculum advisement, and identifying potential drop-outs.

7. A. Satellite offices in residence halls, married housing.

   B. Consultation with dormitory directors and staff, with Disadvantaged Students' Program, and with other university offices.

8. A. Consulting with academic faculties to assist development of better student environment.

   B. Weekly radio program: use students, faculty, discuss current problems, answer questions, and so on.

9. A. Training of student resident assistants for freshman dormitories in advising/quasi-counseling techniques.

   B. Planning and active involvement in program of small group discussions of campus problems, for example, black-white relations; question of interdormitory visitation, campus regulations.

10. A. Director does much advising with Acting President; especially in making him aware of student feelings.

11. A. Consultation groups:
    1. One for the dean of students' staff
    2. Eight for dormitory personnel
    3. Ten for students who help in the dormitory
    4. Two for school and college counselors.

    B. Consultations with faculty:
    1. Members of our staff and the modern language department screen people who are unable to learn foreign language. A program developed by Dinklage at Harvard University.

12. A. Human Relations Workshop approach by two counselors with head residents, assistant heads, and sorority and fraternity housemothers in training program this fall.

    B. Setting up of vocational groups, groups with resident assistants (human relations) and counselors available in halls on open-hour basis during summer and evenings. Have also used staff from associate dean of students' office and placement office as well as counseling center staff.

13. A. Consultation regarding student emotional health with the

majority of colleges on campus and with many university committees and programs including prelaw, premedicine, continuing education, admissions, health center, housing, Indian education, and student union. Rather extensive consultation services are also provided—community school districts, mental health agencies and church groups. We have one person with a half-time office in the student center. We will have this year three persons on half-time basis located in the housing areas.

 B. Providing counseling and consultation services nearer to concentrations of students, such as in the student union and in university housing.

14. A. "Conversations," a series of open discussions held in residence hall. Usually on sex or drugs.

 B. In-service-training group, for student-services staff, including secretaries and deans.

 * N/A This is the first year of operation of the counseling center.

15. A. Training and supervision of a group of undergraduate volunteers who serve as student-to-student counselors, based in the student center. Two members of the professional staff devote at least two hours per week each to this operation.

16. A. Institutional research.

17. A. Outreach to community:
  1. GED Testing Program
  2. Summer program for disadvantaged
  3. Director is member of College-Community Advisory Council
  4. Director is member of Mental Health/Mental Retardation Advisory Board.

 B. Outreach to students:
  1. Roving counselor
  2. Reading and browsing space available to all students
  3. Work with student groups.

18. A. Development of a campus police-student dialogue group led by one of our psychologists consisting of a discussion-encounter group series (four sessions).

 B. Training group for "student advocates" (student ombudsmen—nine in number).

19. A. A rap center that operates each noon hour in our student union. One counselor covers it each day.
20. A. An evening counseling program with professional staff and interns—both individual and group experience available. (A twenty-four-hour crisis/help telephone service is in the mill.)
20. B. Seminars for:
    1. Mature women who are seeking new outlooks or vocations or both (nonstudents)
    2. Contribution of services to the Long Beach Free Clinic (students and nonstudents)
    3. Weekly two-hour luncheon staff conferences with guests from community and campus
    4. Contribution of time in working with minority students especially in helping them acclimate to our campus.
21. A. Involved in Educational Opportunity Program.
22. A. A living-learning unit—coed—which is a direct product of the counseling center. Students have interest in seminars on counseling and will set up student organization, drop-in counseling, information and referral service.
23. No reply.
24. A. Residence halls.
    B. "Listening Ear," a crisis center.
25. A. One-time "warm-up" sessions in residence halls at beginning of terms. Conflict resolution sessions with campus newspaper staff, dormitory officers, and so on.
    B. ESP groups, that is, Effective Study Program, personal development groups.
26. A. Weekend encounter program. Three each semester. (Some are "marathons," most break for sleep Friday and Saturday nights.)
    B. Group counseling in several settings: Residence halls, with residence advisors; E.O.P. students; married couples, "enrichment" program, group counseling, *per se*. (Counseling staff in all instances have taken initiative to form these groups. It takes considerable expenditure of time, thought, and is no problem forming "growth groups"—group counseling for students who come to center and ask for it. We do not consider this outreach.)

27. No reply.
28. No reply.
29. A. We man (in conjunction with student activities) an outreach office for drop-in contact with students. It is a casual place—student government also has space there.

    B. We are consultants to human relations programs of student government. Alternate education programs (very active on our campus last spring after Kent-Cambodia).
    We are available for joint programs with student activities, one with freshman orientation; parent (freshman) orientation; new faculty orientation.

30. A.
    1. Desensitization groups for test taking, anxiety (preventative)
    2. Study skills groups in residence halls (preventative)
    3. Communication skills workshops (preventative)
    4. Couples interaction workshops (preventative) and so forth.

31. A. Assigning counseling staff time for being present in residence halls during specific week nights.

    B. Freeing up time for one counseling staff member to be devoted almost entirely to free circulation among students in the student union facility.

32. A. By student's initiative, formation of dormitory discussion groups to which I am invited.

33. A. Year-long training program for thirty-six student counselors: counseling, drugs, sex, problem pregnancies, security.

    B. All-night phone service: crisis intervention, talk, information, campus.

    C. Night availability for conversations in residence halls.

34. A. Consultation with faculty and administrative in instructional evaluation, and student personnel policy, planning, and operation.

35. A. Community sensitivity programs in churches.

    B. Private practice.

36. A. Free cards passed to new students during orientation—offering:
    FREE guidance and motivation for college success

139

FREE Aptitude Testing and Interpretation as you choose a college major

FREE counseling in all types of personal matters

ALL services in the office of Student Affairs are FREE
—use them according to your needs.

37. A. Supply consulting service, graduate student supervisor and ten tutors to work with disturbed children at local mental health center.

38. A. Free Volunteer Tutorial Program: Students volunteer to tutor any other students in courses they have received a B or A in. A service citation is given to students who tutor.

39. A. Counselors go weekly to a prison to counsel prisoners who are taking college extension classes.
    B. We run group meetings for persons in New Career Programs at their place of employment.

40. A. Subcenter in living-learning complex.
    B. Drug education.

41. A. Hotline.
    B. Developing a growth center concept out of the counseling center.

42. A. Dormitory consultation.
    B. Telephone counseling service.

43. A. Personnel growth groups for campus organizations such as Baptist Student Union.

44. A. A group of concerned students at Franklin and Marshall College have started a peer counseling program for drug users. They have facilities in the counseling center and are under the supervision of the counseling center staff. Presently, they are in operation on Friday, Saturday and Sunday eves. These students are attempting to provide two types of service. First, they are attempting to help the student who is using or is considering the use of drugs to assess his motivation. It is our hope they will help the student more accurately assess why he is using drugs and what effect they are having on him. Second, they are attempting to help the student on a bad trip by providing support and attempting to direct the individual to the College Health Service where he can receive proper medical care.

Outreach Functions Performed by College Counseling Centers

45. A. Liaison with nearby School of Medicine whereby psychiatric residents use our facility for training and jointly developed program in family therapy.
    B. Referral source for nearby small private university which has limited counseling center facilities.
46. A. Three of us engage in work with handicapped children.
    B. Occasional talks to parent and professional groups.
47. A. Dormitory counselor training sessions.
48. A. Coordination of academic advisements for "undecided majors" each quarter for almost 400 students out of 5,700 enrollment.
    B. Counseling with approximately 200 "summer trial" program students who are poor academic risks. They are seen individually or in small groups at least once.
    C. Conducting How to Study session in the dormitories for all interested students, especially those who are on academic probation.
    D. Serving as resource people for Counselor Training Program at this institution.
    E. Working as staff advisor for a major council in student government.
49. A. Communication skills training to allied health programs:
       1. Physical therapists
       2. Mental health assistants
       3. Pediatrician aids.
    B. Classroom examination workshops for faculty.
    C. Drug information services.
50. A. Emotional-social problems growing out of dormitory and off-campus housing privileges, that is, ways in which the values and patterns vary. Center staff is engaged in group counseling involving men and women students.
51. A. Several sensitivity groups run by our staff (which usually turn out to be group therapy).
    B. Talks at orientation of new students and resident assistants.
52. A. Work with resident hall personnel.
    B. Participation in training students to help in the Community Crisis Center.
53. A. Residence hall visitation by all staff on a regular basis.
    B. Inviting by letter new entrants to come in for familiarization orientation.

54. A. We are assisting in training LGAs (Living Group Advisors) for the resident halls.
    B. We have a counselor-at-large who operates mainly on the campus as a whole. He helps people where the problems are.
55. A. Instituted a new class (credit) for resident counselors in residence halls.
    B. Consult with faculty and staff with reference to research pertaining to student characteristics.
56. A. One staff counselor housed in the School of Business for referral. Also three three-quarter-time people housed in residence halls for referral from residence hall staff and for inservice training with same staff.
    B. Two staff members serve as consultants to House for Human Growth, operated by the Guidance and Counseling Department. One in group work and one general.
57. A. Counselors from center spend a half-day per week in a counseling office in a residence hall.
    B. Counselors act as consultants to groups of students who need assistance in solving concerns with college adjustment.
58. A. We have two staff and two or three graduate assistants spending much time with drug problems, hippies, and related groups.
59. A. Improvement of faculty advising. Counselor works as consultant to faculty, conducts in-service training regarding counseling-oriented approaches to students, and coordinates efforts at enhancing faculty-student relationships.
60. A. Leadership training for new student program leaders, freshman seminar paraprofessionals, student government officers, pledge trainers, and so on.
    B. Study of student development research project including feedback to the campus re the data.
61. A. Crisis Phone Service staffed by trained volunteers.
    B. Drug Drop-in Center: drug education program to start winter quarter, 1971.
62. No reply.
63. A. Drug education program in residence halls. Presently attempting to establish a peer drug counseling program.
    B. A required precollege counseling program for all entering freshmen. We feel this is our major source of getting students

to avail themselves of our counseling services throughout their years of college.

64. A. Couples' workshops. For those going together, engaged, living together, and married. Exceptionally valuable and rewarding, to them and us. Workshops are experiential, process-oriented, emphasis and skill development of an interpersonal nature. We are training faculty husbands and wives for leading these groups, and some married students.

64. B. Paraprofessional counseling: crisis center (drugs, loneliness); draft counseling; sexuality (education, abortion, and so on). Just getting off the ground on this one.

65. A. Consultation in dormitories with student advisers or groups of students.

   B. Supervision of Peer Counseling Unit.

66. A. Biweekly sessions with residence hall assistants for discussions.

67. A. We have our junior staff living-out in off-campus housing "student ghetto"—rent and phone is paid by the university. Mental health education for special groups, for instance, premeds.

   B. Our senior staff does not routinely engage in ongoing counseling (except groups). Are used for: consultation; teaching; program development; community action. A trio now deciding who should leave school (as consultants). "Most effort is for least disturbed."

68. A. Challenge '70: Challenge is a series of round-table meetings being held during the fall semester at Madison College with the initial thrust during orientation. The groups focus on particular issues, concerns, topics or ideas that are relevant to today's students. Designed to foster thought, analysis, discussion and communication, the program provides a unique opportunity for students and faculty to confront a central topic and deal with it in a meaningful manner. The program's objectives are approached through a series of small group discussions, panel discussions, and informal conversations.

   B. Resident Hall Advising Program: During the past year, the counseling center staff expanded their involvement in the ongoing training of the residence hall assistants. The program was initiated by a "micro marathon" sensitivity session structured to increase self-awareness as a preliminary step to the

143

teaching of responses which tend to facilitate the growth of human beings. Periodic meetings were held throughout the year with the men and women resident assistants in an attempt to provide continuous training and to maintain a high level of motivation regarding the needs of students residing in dormitories. The impact of this program was thoroughly evaluated by the professional staff of the office of student affairs, and plans for expanded involvement and additional training were completed for the 1970–71 academic year.

69. A. Resident Hall Assistants In-Service Training Program: formal and informal discussions (rap sessions with assistants and residents).

B. Staff psychologist at large on campus two evenings per week in addition to availability during day to meet with students, for example, Latin American student group.

70. A. No specific program as such. Numerous speaking engagements to various organizations both on campus and off.

71. A. In-service training with resident counselors of the Weekend College Program (a division funded under Model Cities for disadvantaged minorities).

B. Operation of study skills seminars in conjunction with reading laboratory staff for evening students.

72. A. The several branch offices of the center, located strategically on campus, continue to provide traditional services geared to specific needs related to the geographic areas they serve, but also are developing considerable innovations in resident assistant training, developmental groups for students, consultation services for faculty, and in the conduct of workshops for various groups such as student scholarship committees, residence hall advisory staff, faculty members in the semi-autonomous colleges, and religious advisors. Additionally, such programming is increasingly incorporated into the training of interns and practicum students. Liaison work with an off-campus crisis intervention center, and with a drug education center has developed this past year.

B. One major type of outreach program begun this past year has been oriented toward minority students. This has included the appointment of an Assistant Director for minority student counseling and the establishment of a branch office in the student union building oriented toward minority student needs. This center goes well beyond the provision of traditional services and reaches minority students through a variety of channels, both formal and informal.

73. A. Support program for economically disadvantaged students.
    B. Residence hall staff in-service training.
74. A. Meet with residence hall advisors in small groups to consult on problems.
    B. Meet with all other college student personnel workers for a consultation meeting.
75. A. Lunch-hour (eleven to two) availability of a counselor four days per week at the student center in a specified room with a relaxed setting.
    B. Small group sessions with disadvantaged students in their first few weeks at the college.
    C. Group conferences with half-sections of freshman class during the fall.
76. A. Consultants to residence hall counselors.
77. A. None that seem to fit the name as we interpret it.
78. A. Crisis telephone service after office hours, operated cooperatively with two area colleges; manned by student volunteers. Staffs of three counseling centers responsible for training of volunteers and coordination of effort.
79. A. Providing consultation to dormitory counselors (students) and residents (staff).
80. A. No difference from that reported last year.
81. A. University College Liaison: One counselor has been assigned one-half time to coordinate the center's contacts with University College in which all freshmen spend their first academic year. The liaison counselor arranges speakers to explain counseling services at the freshman survey courses, meets with the UVC academic advisers, and serves as a contact for referrals from the advisers. Career planning groups for freshmen have also been arranged through the liaison counselor.
    B. Residence hall consultants: Three counselors are assigned to the residence hall area—one each for three geographic areas. These counselors spend 80 per cent of their time in the residence halls as consultants to the residence hall staff, also as-

sisting in staff training, conducting groups, and occasionally seeing students. These counselors spend 20 per cent of their time in regular, direct counseling service at the counseling center.

82. A. Consulting about development of and coordination of telephone crises center with walk-in service as possibility.

B. Again and again and again trying to instigate meaningful drug education program re illicit drugs, abuse of legal drugs, alcohol, and tobacco.

83. A. Each counselor is assigned one day a week to a specific residence hall to do counseling—the same as if he was in the office in the center. This allows us contact with students who would not come to the center. It also allows close liaison with hall staff and student assistants. Referrals from these sources have increased in quantity and quality.

B. A program is being developed in coordination with cultural chairmen in residence halls. It involves the counselors' conducting discussions on topics chosen by students (for example, drugs, abortion, vocational choice). Two or three floors of a hall would be combined for such a session. Each topic is thoroughly researched by the counselors before an attempt is made at discussion.

84. No reply.

85. A. Residence Hall Liaison Program in which each counselor maintains contact with a residence hall. He (she) may work with staff, meet with small groups, and talk with floor groups. One counselor also works with residence halls administrative staff on training, and so forth.

B. Counselors work with a number of committees involved with student concerns such as educational opportunities committee, new student program committee, Head Advisors Committee, and minority student admissions committee.

86. A. Consultation to residence hall staff.

B. Teaching study skills course.

87. A. Outreach to disadvantaged students for twenty hours per week to work on a one-to-one basis in reading and study skills.

B. Counseling disadvantaged and minority students in settings other than, but not necessarily exclusive of, the traditional offices. Also using new approaches to counseling by getting

146

involved with the students in special programs and in student gathering places, that is, cafeteria, student centers, and so on.

88. A. No reply.
89. A. Consultation and involvement with the office for black student affairs.
    B. Crisis Intervention Telephone Service.
90. A. Freelancing; whereby counselors spend one-half of each day out of office circulating in student traffic areas, such as lounges, and recreation areas. The number of client/contacts made are inestimably high and worthwhile investments of time.
    B. On a rotating schedule, a counselor mans a drop-in post within the dormitory complex during week nights. Seems to be meeting a need, though sometimes sporadic use demands periodic reevaluation.
91. A. One counselor (not counted in center staff) detached to dormitory during evening hours.
    B. One counselor is informal advisor to unofficial group of students serving as bad trip and crisis helpers.
92. A. Ad hoc committee on the drug scene—composed of students, chaplain, dean of students, and counseling psychologists—to establish drug library available to all students; discuss other means of education; establish lines of referral of problems; explore policies and programs on other campuses, and so on.
    B. Orientation of dormitory counselors and staff re emotional and other student problems, and specific aid in interpreting vocational tests.
93. A. Availability of counselors in the residence halls—three to five hours a week in each hall.
    B. Preregistration and registration advising in various parts of the campus.
    C. Participation with other student personnel services in providing general advising and referral service to students in their major department physical facility.
94. A. Attempts to establish more involvement with residence halls, financial aids, and associated students.
    B. Working as teachers of general studies seminars.
95. A. Operation of a twenty-four-hour crisis line that the counseling center answers during the day and an answering service

answers at night. One counselor is responsible for crisis calls on any given night.

B. Coordination of a Coping with Reality Program including the training of student and faculty group facilitators. This program delves into facts, fictions, attitudes, perceptions, and values of students using drugs, alcohol, sexual behavior, withdrawal as ways of escaping from reality.

96. A. We have our counselors available in all dormitories two to three hours per week working as consultants mainly with resident assistants.

B. We attend many meetings on campus of faculty and students. Right now, in connection with a university-wide self-study program.

97. A. Setting up and running a variety of groups, for example, human awareness laboratories.

B. Acting as a consultant for the dormitory resident assistants and faculty in a variety of group situations.

98. A. Human relations training and leadership training programs for individuals and student groups.

B. Consultation with faculty on the design of innovative courses and programs.

99. A. Group counseling for disadvantaged admitted under an open admission program (federally funded) utilizing not only counseling staff but administrators too.

B. Sensitivity program geared to leadership training for officers of clubs.

100. A. Image of Women Program which alerts undergraduate to work in which women can develop an identity through career choice and combining the roles.

B. Consultation to house counselors in the dormitory.

101. A. Serving as clearing house-coordination center to place student volunteers (whom we recruit) in various community agencies who ask for help of various kinds.

B. Recruitment of "mature students"—planning ahead after forty, especially women.

102. A. Directing student outreach service training (on continual basis) students to counsel other students who walk in to the SOS office. A twenty-four-hour telephone service is also run by this office.

B. Initiating new undergraduate programs.

Outreach Functions Performed by College Counseling Centers

103.   A. With city school elementary school students—twenty-two children. We are conducting achievement motivation therapy.

   B. We have just received funds for a Title 1 project for a Mobile Guidance Center for Orangeburg County Target, population: 1,000 junior and senior high students—object: to cut the drop-out rate. $30,126 Federal, $19,667 contributing cost.

104.   A. Freshman Advisor Program: We supervise, administer, and coordinate faculty advisors to freshmen.

   B. Tutorial Program: We oversee a student tutorial program, with tutoring done by upperclass students.

   C. Reading Program: During the summer for incoming freshmen.

105.   A. Developmental Skills Program for disadvantaged urban blacks and rural whites.

   B. Drug Crisis Center and now an all Crisis and Psychological Information Center is being developed.

   C. Satellite centers.

   D. Classes in interpersonal relations, vocational choice, and personal adjustment.

106.   A. Faculty evaluation, test scoring, and consultation services.

   B. Consultants to various campus groups. Students, resident assistant training, and so on.

107.   A. Growth groups for resident assistants in residence halls.

   B. Groups involving explorations in: human potential; premarriage enrichment; human sexuality; loneliness; religious values.

108.   A. Counselor-at-large: more informal contacts in student center, residence halls, at student activities, and so on.

   B. University committees: Admissions and Credits Committee; Faculty Senate; Advisor–Student Association Senate; Curriculum Revision Committee; Health Services Committee; Fraternity Advisor.

109.   A. No reply.
   Note: Increased case load with no increase in staff has resulted in discontinuance of some out-of-center activities reported last year.

110.   No reply.

111.   No reply.

112.   A. Counselor-loan program: Each professional counselor spends one-half day per week in each of the residence halls. Co-

ordination of the program is effected through monthly meetings involving the personnel deans, head residents, and staff of the Counseling and Testing Center.

113. No reply.

114. A. Summer Freshman Orientation in Emotional Education: Frosh volunteer to come to campus for one of six groups—150 students for two and a half days. Year training of faculty and student personnel staff to handle small groups. Program consisted of microlaboratories, encounter groups, vocational and personal planning, and decision making. Research of results in progress.

B. In-service training of student personnel staff (Master Degree, counselor oriented). Cocounseling, encounter group, case staffing and consultation about their counselees.

115. A. We have asked to serve on (Faculty, Student, Administration) Committee on Student Life. This group serves as policy-making and judicial branches of university influencing campus atmosphere. We also instigated Advisory Committee composed of deans, health center personnel, religious chaplains, and counselors to coordinate helping services available.

B. We have offered our services as referral sources to crisis telephone student group.

116. A. Work with academic officers (students, cadets) in cadet squadrons to help them provide study skills assistance to academically weak cadets within their squadrons. (Squadrons are small groups of students living in close proximity—somewhat akin to a fraternity perhaps.)

B. Consultation with various other agencies concerning programs to provide career information, study assistance, and personal assistance to cadets.

117. A. Training volunteers for crisis-line, recently inagurated in town.

118. A. We now have three counselors working in the dormitories, conducting groups and establishing relationships. In some of these groups we are training dormitory counselors to improve their counseling skills, other groups are open to dormitory residents in general.

B. We are supervising the student effort to provide after-hours telephone emergency counseling.

119. No reply.

150

Outreach Functions Performed by College Counseling Centers

120. A. Crisis Center: Manned and administered by students. We helped initiate program, selected and trained volunteers, participated in advisory capacity and as a referral source (university community).
   B. Drug Information Center: Provided training for drug center "leaders" and participated on their Professional Advisory Council (city community).
   C. Nurses' Residence: Provided "get acquainted" training laboratories, and introduction to counseling service personnel. Provided a roving counselor.
121. A. Development of social program for older students, graduates, and seniors over twenty-one, initiated by a counseling center staff member.
   B. Liaison with academic units, both colleges and professional schools, along with regular counseling staff meetings with a faculty or administrative representative.
   C. Orientations: Policy making and participation.
122. A. "The House?": A peer counseling or student counseling project. We are training the students on that staff.
   B. Training via an education department course, a group of student personnel workers on campus, such as EOP counselors (minority), assistant dean of women, and so on.
   C. Training students for group leaders of structured, low-risk, task-oriented groups.
   D. Introducing educational innovative ideas—such as a plan for a human potential college which is built around a work-study, quarter-off idea.
   E. Weekend retreats—being facilitators for faculty-student retreats. (We used to do this, abandoned it, but plan to begin again.)
   F. Building a fire under the faculty advising system where we can. Encouraging a student academic advising program.
123. A. Center staff present in residence halls, on campus and off.
   B. Consultation with student groups.
124. A. Walk-in offices in residence halls.
   B. Seminars for student service staffs and faculty.
125. A. Satellite office in adjacent student community of Isla Vista. Large enough for one group, one personal counseling. Open two to ten p.m., four days per week.

151

B. Marriage counseling for couples in off-campus quarters, one morning per week.

126. A. Special counselor-training program for resident assistants and head residents.

B. "Warm room" drop-in counseling service manned by students and supervised by counselors.

C. Decentralized offices—one in each college.

127. A. Created minority student counseling satellite unit in student union.

B. Started psychology service in student health service.

128. A. Consultation to dormitory counselors and resident assistants. Rather this than students. We feel that we can reach more students this way.

B. We have also gone to a workshop concept—marriage counseling; anxiety and test-taking; vocational decision making; and so on.

129. A. Direct involvement of staff members in compensatory pre-college program for "high-risk" students; time for out-of-office follow-up with those students.

B. Cooperative effort (primarily with resident hall staff) to reach low-achieving freshmen in their dormitories.

130. A. A counselor is assigned to each of the conventional residence halls and is available one evening a week for walk-ins and staff consultation. Another is assigned to apartment halls, working with groups of students and staff. Yet another is conducting group marriage counseling in married student housing.

B. Counselors also serve as advisors to the open clinic (mostly drugs and birth control information), and participate in the selection and training of students who operate a help line; counselors are also on call for help line appeals beyond the skill of the students.

131. A. We plan a Vocational Development Conference for resident hall students.

B. Test-anxiety groups set up in halls conducted by residence hall personnel.

132. A. One staff member has taken responsibility for liaison with housing department personnel working with their director on program development as well as directly with residence hall

counselors in a consultative capacity. Prior to the opening of school this fall, eight staff members took part as group facilitators in a two-day workshop involving residence hall counselors.

B. One staff member with a primary interest in sense awareness and growth groups is offering a series of three of both type groups this fall quarter. Preliminary research and experience has conducted last school year to determine response and desirability of this type activity. All such groups are on a voluntary basis (the student makes application), and students are informed of the nature and intent of the expected group experience. Sense awareness groups are composed of thirty to fifty students who meet in a residence hall auditorium daily for five days for a two-hour period. Growth groups are composed of from ten to sixteen students who meet for approximately twelve hours in a single day.

133. A. Undergraduate paraprofessional program. Hotline (drug and suicide); training dormitory resident assistants and selection; working with high school and secondary schools in group work; campus politics; exit interviewing; working with transfer students.

B. Our interns (four) visit various campus and off-campus agencies and hopefully are able to work in several for one or two weeks.

134. A. Training undergraduate interviewers to use standardized interview technique who roam campus interviewing on a different topic every two weeks. Interviews are anonymous, but information helps administration keep abreast of student attitudes and feelings while students see counseling center as visible and involved.

B. Training and supervision of black and Mexican American student groups for recruitment in selected high schools.

135. A. Training resident assistants (dormitory).

B. Mock interview and follow-up interviews for all premeds, preparing for medical school interviews.

C. Training agricultural county agents.

136. A. We are a center for G.E.D. which tests hundreds of community persons.

B. Have a summer counselor program. Counselors (black, Latin)

153

from high schools in area are hired for a two-month period in the summer.

137. A. Consultation with dormitories and campus groups by the staff.
B. Vocational interest groups in dormitories and in off-campus housing.
C. Study skills group in union for interested students.
D. Sex education groups in the dormitories and women's resident halls.

138. A. Participation in staff development by member of our staff with other student affairs people.
B. Participation in a rotating (three-way) internship for the clinical psychology trainees of the University of Kentucky.

139. A. Orientation and follow-up activities with dormitory resident assistants.

140. A. Consultation to faculty and administrators re student problems and administration. Procedures (admissions, and so on).
B. Course proposals for:
1. Communications
2. Psychology of university teaching.

141. A. Residence hall consultation.
B. Ongoing group with members of student activity's professional staff.

142. A. Drug education and drop-in center staffed by paraprofessionals (students). We developed this jointly with the Health Service and Dean of Students Office over the past year.
B. A training program for secretaries in awareness of self and interpersonal skills.

143. A. Parents' Orientation seminar during summer orientation program.
B. Case consultation with dormitory staff.

144. No reply.

145. A. Working with noncredit seminar to develop sex information service for students—use of counseling facilities involved.
B. Helping interested students develop skills as "draft counselors," and arranging facilities and time for student-to-student services in this area.

146. A. Consultation with faculty, deans, housing, campus security.
B. We plan to train all academic advisors in the spring of 1971.

Outreach Functions Performed by College Counseling Centers

147. A. An outreach program in staffing "New Hamlin House," a center for the counterculture, hippies, and drug abusers.
    B. Taking group training outside the center to the dormitories, sororities and fraternities in study skills, vocational decisions, sex education, communication, and social skills.

148. A. Working with two fraternities toward developing a more effective scholastic program.
    B. Developing an advance placement program for the university.

149. A. Use of students as vocational and career counselors.
    B. Use of alumni as career counselors to seniors.

150. A. Training of dormitory and other living-group resident assistants.
    B. V.A. counseling contract.

151. A. Development of a Teaching and Learning Center resource to faculty (through faculty teaching council) for the improvement of undergraduate education.
    B. Newsletter to faculty: *Focus on Student Development.*
       Newsletter to selected students: *Student Focus.*

152. A. Group work with resident assistants in dormitory.
    B. Using test information for recruiting top students and using test information to bring faculty up to date on students.

153. A. Consultation to student-run crisis clinic, resident assistants, faculty, and staff.
    B. Training of interviewers for research purposes.

154. A. Requiring students on probation to come in and review their present academic standing.
    B. Consulting, that is, making oneself available to other offices, agencies, minority studies programs, and so on.

155. No reply.

156. A. Students initiated a seven p.m. to seven a.m. drop-in and phone center (RAP). Center assisted by providing training seminars and faculty advisor role and consultation and referral resource.
    B. Center staff have participated in group interaction training with students in nursing and in physical education.
    C. Center has been involved in helping Indian students establish a cultural center.

155

157. A. Supervision and training of students who use hotline or crisis intervention center on the campus.

B. Reach Out program: Counselors led discussion with great assistance from students who have been on drugs to assist other students in moving away from excessive drug usage.

158. A. Visits to residence halls by counselors (no satellite centers yet).

B. Nonverbal encounter groups (Union Policy Board and some instructional classes in communication).

C. Instructional classes (presentations).

159. A. Establishment of a field office in a dormitory adjacent to a black concentration and staffed by two black counselors. Focus groups on frustrations of hall life are also connected with this. These have the effectiveness of communication laboratories for black and white students.

B. Intensive human relations training provided to students' leadership of one dormitory with a good deal of consultation to support these leaders. A concentrated effort is being made on a demonstration basis to upgrade the "human environment" of this hall. Consultation is also provided to the professional staff of this hall.

160. A. Consulting with graduate and undergraduate students who work as counselors in the dormitories. We are available to all of them for regular group consultation. About ten currently use us. We will expand this if our client load decreases.

B. Regular training-consultation with staff of Crisis Center, a student-run operation providing phone and walk-in help to anyone in the university community. The center is open from six p.m. to six a.m. About 50 per cent of its clientele are on bad drug trips, the other 50 per cent have emotional problems, a few are suicidal.

161. A. We don't have what I consider an outreach program. We have one or two in mind after attending last year's Directors Conference.

162. A. Black counseling interns who counsel informally outside office (roving counselors).

B. Career seminars: Persons representing various careers are invited to the campus for informal discussion with students.

163. A. Periodic events: films, panels, debates—about two a year.

156

B. Consultation, orientation, group discussion with minority students.

164. A. Freshman orientation follow-up, group guidance, small group test interpretation. Strong vocational blank administered to all freshmen.

B. Reading and study skills program in which anyone from freshmen to doctoral-level professors are participants.

C. Active involvement in facilitation training with student groups; weekend retreats, and so on.

D. Plans for weekly vocational article in school newspaper.

E. Plans for participation in Math Department, one credit orientation course.

F. Direct participation in disadvantaged student programs—board and special services for disadvantaged.

165. A. Work closely with campus clergy in their related counseling role and function.

B. Developed a training program for the undergraduate resident assistants to better prepare them for their respective roles and functions in student life.

166. A. Paraprofessional credit courses for resident hall staff.

B. Satellite services include twenty-four hours' availability for consultation in resident halls.

167. A. Periodic in-service sessions with undergraduate counselors and graduate staff residents in residence halls. This is poorly organized. Our contact with these people seems to threaten other administrators under whom they work. There seems to be a fear of divided loyalty.

B. The active participation of two counselors (one of them the director) in community and campus organization. The director has been active in mental health associations for over ten years. The other counselor is advisor to an honor society and a religious group.

168. A. Small encounter group training sessions with staff and students' resident assistants in many of the residence halls.

B. Married Student Counseling Service provided in large married student housing apartment (on a part-time basis). Individual and couple counseling on a short-term and crisis basis. Also married student groups.

169. A. A major outreach activity on our campus is the training of a

network of helping people such as campus chaplains, faculty members, and student personnel staff, according to the systematic Human Relation Training Model.

B. Another important outreach activity is the coordination of a program in vocational awareness and job opportunities with specific academic departments.

170. A. Consultation to a new coed residence hall on campus where the consultant has access to the director of the dormitory, to her immediate supervisor and to student advisors.

B. Telephone Counseling and Referral Service, whose contacts were not reported in the body of this report, but whose usage has increased tremendously and is part of the Counseling-Psychological Services Center's operation. The total number of calls for the year 1969–70 was 31,824, which was almost a 62 per cent increase of usage of this outreach service from the year 1969.

171. A. Involvement with residence hall staff: advising, consulting, group work.

B. Advisory and consulting role with respective groups: that is, chaplain corps; student programming; same community agency, area involvement.

172. A. Doctoral-level staff member schedules four hours per week in office provided by College of Medicine (which is somewhat isolated from rest of campus). Sees medical students experiencing stress, having personal-family problems, and so on.

B. Residence hall program: Head resident in dormitories (who is doctoral candidate in counseling psychology program) has joint appointment as intern in counseling center. He coordinates our services, sees dormitory residents, and so on.

173. A. Consultant-advisorship to student-operated drug crisis center.

B. Sensitivity groups with first-year nursing students prior to their initiating live contact with patient.

174. A. We are involved as individuals in informal things: committees on human relations; an undergraduate seminar on communication problems; teaching a course on parent effectiveness; consulting with student and faculty groups; a committee to develop a student-run drug counseling and crash pad; meeting occasionally with residence hall counselors on special

problems; helping the student run YMCA interview candidates for community involvement programs, and so on.

B. We have no present outreach program of a deliberate nature at this time.

175. A. Consultation with Campus Plunge and Orientation program based on Plunge Model. (Conflict inducement-resolution model.) Including director and family living in residence hall throughout summer (three days each week).

B. Regular consultation with residence hall staff, special education counseling staff, university YMCA—YWCA professional staff.

176. A. Satellite officer.

B. Rap room.

C. Telephone counseling.

D. International student peer counseling.

E. Residence consulting.

F. Forum, panels, and so on.

G. Consultative committee.

H. High school liaison work.

I. "Dorm-tour" committee involvement.

177. A. Work with men's residence halls.

178. A. Student Support Program: Forty-one upperclassmen work in supportive roles with new students. SDC staff supervises, trains, evaluates program.

B. Hotline: twenty-four-hour emergency service—makes counselors accessible to students when they meet them at night and weekends.

179. A. Teacher effectiveness evaluated campuswide.

B. National Drug Education Training Program: thirteen states and the Virgin Islands.

180. A. Office hours in Student Health Center.

B. Office hours in residence halls.

181. A. Each staff member spends one evening a week in a residence hall, where hall staff and students may contact him or her for group or individual conferences.

B. Doctoral staff members have participated in a community program, serving as trainers for volunteer workers who will serve as telephone listeners and referral agents for persons seeking information and assistance.

159

    C. Also, during the past two years, an informal course in self-hypnosis has been offered to interested undergraduate and graduate students.

182. A. Training programs (T-groups) for residence hall counselors as an ongoing project.

183. No reply.

184. A. Low-level, open-ended discussion groups in the residence halls. As initially conceived, one member of the staff plus one invited faculty member conducted each of these groups. Our goal was to shift responsibility for this group concept to the deans and dormitory counselors in order to free our staff once it was going. We were successful for two years. This year we may have to reinitiate the groups because they are not yet running this year.

    B. Drug Education Center: A former client (who said he resented the way in which the hospital handled him following a bad trip) set up a twenty-four-hour, seven-day-a-week center off campus for walk-ins on bad trips and the usual things. We consulted with him in setting it up; one staff member is on the professional advisory board, and a junior staff member (the psychometrist) volunteers one night a week there.

    C. In general, our goal in outreach has been to facilitate the development of services outside the center for which we will have minimal financial and supervisory responsibility. "Involve Others" is our outreach motto.

185. A. Consultant to residence hall staff which includes staff in-service training, talk to student, availability by phone to head resident day or night for question answering.

    B. Emergency consultant to health service physician on night call. The physician has a roster of center staff available to call if he wants assistance in a psychiatric emergency case.

186. A. Much informal contact through consultation and joint appointments with dormitory staffs. This includes individual and group consultation. In 1970–71, a walk-in counseling and consulting service has been established in the dormitory area, staffed by one present and two former members of counseling service staff.

187. A. Sponsorship of student telephone contact service (Hi-Line).

Outreach Functions Performed by College Counseling Centers

188. A. Special counseling of marginal admission students on academic probation.
    B. Information-referral service.
189. A. Members of this office helped establish and serve as consultants to a half-way house for persons who have recovered from a psychiatric episode that required hospitalization.
    B. Members of this office helped secure fundings for a teenage center in the city of Middletown and serve as a professional resource to the college students who are involved as administrators and workers.
190. No reply.
191. A. Contact with student groups to explain our services.
    B. Consulting work by staff members with members of residence hall staffs.
192. No reply.
193. A. Crisis Center. This is run by students for people who need help with drugs. They may go for other help but it is for drugs. The students are referred to other sources for additional help.
194. A. A pilot program with the Music Department to ascertain the effect of group counseling experiences on the recital performances of undergraduate vocal music majors.
195. No reply.
196. A. Seminar series for campus ministers (an informal get-together); we try to rotate to each other's facilities.
    B. Advised local youth in their development of an emergency phone system.
197. A. Scheduled contacts within residence halls of full-time counselors.
    B. Visitation within local hospitals of any university student admitted.
198. A. Satellite offices in residence halls.
    B. Group counseling with resident assistants, nurses, and underachievers.
199. A. Every week each member of the counseling staff is assigned to be in a particular dormitory on campus. Consequently, each of the dormitories has a counselor in the dormitory for three hours a week. He is assigned to work with the resident assistants, discuss dormitory activities with the directors, and

161

see any of the counselees that stop into his outreach office. If any dormitory problems arise when the counselor is not in his outreach office, dormitory personnel and students are encouraged to contact the outreach counselor to their dormitory as opposed to contacting the counseling center for any of the counselors.

    B. Three members of the staff are acting as resource consulting personnel to the emergency answering service that has been established by the students on campus.

200. A. Counseling availability in university colleges.

201. A. Selection, in-service training, and ongoing consultation with resident advisees.

    B. Orientation (freshmen): testing and interpretation.

202. No reply.

203. A. College program: Offers a consultant function to faculty, staff, and student groups or individuals. Try to improve the ecology of the college through goal-setting meetings with the above. Provide orientation to all members of the college re programs offered by central service. Provide specific contact person for each college. Provide some individual and group counseling service for college members.

204. A. Tutorial program for disadvantaged students.

    B. Developmental groups for high-achieving students.

Bibliography

ALBERT, G. "A Survey of College Counseling Facilities." *Personnel and Guidance Journal*, 1968, *46*, 540–543.

ALTMAN, R. A., AND SNYDER, P. O. (Eds.) *The Minority Student on the Campus: Expectations and Possibilities*. Boulder, Colo.: Center for Research and Development in Higher Education and Western Interstate Commission for Higher Education, 1971.

BISNO, H. "Professional Status and Professional Policies: A Heterodox Analysis." *Counseling News and Views*, 1960, *12*(3), 4–11.

BOROW, H. (Ed.) *Man in a World of Work*. Boston: Houghton Mifflin, 1964.

CARKHUFF, R. R., AND BERENSON, B. G. *Beyond Counseling and Therapy*. New York: Holt, Rinehart, and Winston, 1967.

CARTER, T. P. *Mexican Americans in School: A History of Educational Neglect*. New York: College Entrance Examination Board, 1970.

CASSARA, B. B. (Ed.) *American Women: The Changing Image*. Boston: Beacon, 1962.

CHICKERING, A. W. *Education and Identity*. San Francisco: Jossey-Bass, 1969.

CLARK, D. D. "Characteristics of Counseling Centers in Large Universities." *Personnel and Guidance Journal,* 1966, *44,* 817–823.

DANSKIN, D. G. "The University and a Fully Functioning Counseling Center: A Theoretical Viewpoint." Speech at the American Personnel and Guidance Association Convention, Las Vegas, 1969.

DANSKIN, D. G., AND KENNEDY, C. E. "Student Services in Higher Education: What Are Student Services?" Unpublished manuscript, Kansas State University, 1969.

ELLMAN, M. *Thinking About Women.* New York: Harcourt Brace Jovanovich, 1968.

FELDMAN, K. A., AND NEWCOMB, T. M. *The Impact of College on Students.* San Francisco: Jossey-Bass, 1969.

FOLGER, J. K., ASTIN, H. S., AND BOYER, A. E. *Human Resources and Higher Education.* New York: Russell Sage Foundation, 1970.

FOULDS, M. L., AND GUINAN, J. F. "On Becoming a Growth Center." *The Journal of College Student Personnel,* 1970, *11,* 177–181.

GALLAGHER, P. J., AND DEMOS, G. D. *The Counseling Center in Higher Education.* Springfield, Ill.: Thomas, 1970.

GOLDSCHMID, M. L. (Ed.) *Black Americans and White Racism: Theory and Research.* New York: Holt, Rinehart, and Winston, 1970.

GORDON, J. E. "Project Cause: The Federal Anti-Poverty Program and Some Implications of Sub-Professional Training." *American Psychologist,* 1965, *20*(5), 333–343.

HALLECK, S. L. *The Politics of Therapy.* New York: Science House, 1971.

HARPER, F. D. "Black Student Revolt on White Campuses," *The Journal of College Student Personnel.* 1969, *10,* 292–295.

HEATH, D. H. *Growing Up in College.* San Francisco: Jossey-Bass, 1968.

HEIST, P. (Ed.), *The Creative College Student: An Unmet Challenge.* San Francisco: Jossey-Bass, 1968.

HOBBS, L. *Love and Liberation: Up Front with the Feminists.* New York: McGraw-Hill, 1970.

HODGKINSON, H. H. "How Deans of Students Are Seen by Others— and Why." *NASPA Journal,* 1970, *8,* 49–54.

KIRK, B., AND OTHERS. "Guidelines for University and College Counseling Services." *American Psychologist,* 1971, *26,* 585–589.

KOILE, E. A. "The Faculty and the University Counseling Center." *Journal of Counseling Psychology,* 1960, *7,* 293–297.

Bibliography

LETCHWORTH, G. C. "Women Who Return to College: An Identity-Integrity Approach," *The Journal of College Student Personnel,* 1970, *11,* 103–106.

LIFTON, R. J. (Ed.) *The Woman in America.* Boston: Houghton Mifflin, 1965.

MC LEAN, P. E. "A Study of Organizational Administrative Practices and Policies Characterizing Student Counseling Centers in Selected U. S. Colleges and Universities." Unpublished manuscript. Texas A and I University, 1967.

MAGOON, T. M. College Centers Annual Data Bank. Thermofax. University of Maryland, 1970.

MOORE, W., JR. *Against the Odds.* San Francisco: Jossey-Bass, 1970.

MORGAN, G. D. *The Ghetto College Student: A Descriptive Essay on College Youth from the Inner City.* Iowa City, Iowa: The American College Testing Program, 1970.

MUELLER, K. H. *Student Personnel Work in Higher Education.* Boston: Houghton Mifflin, 1961.

OETTING, E. R., IVEY, A. E., AND WIEGEL, R. G. *The College and University Counseling Center.* Washington, D. C.: American Personnel and Guidance Association. Monograph 11, 1970.

OSIPOW, S. H. *Theories of Career Development.* New York: Appleton-Century-Crofts, 1968.

PATTERSON, C. H. "Some Problems and Proposals in College Counseling." In HESTON, J. C., AND FRICK, W. V. (Eds.) *The Professional Preparation of Counseling Psychologists.* New York: Teachers College Bureau of Publications, 1964.

PATTERSON, C. H. "The Social Responsibility of Psychology." *The Counseling Psychologist,* 1969a, *1*(4), 97–100.

PATTERSON, C. H. "What is Counseling Psychology?" *Journal of Counseling Psychology,* 1969b, *16,* 23–29.

PENNEY, J. F. "Student Personnel Work: A Profession Stillborn." *Personnel and Guidance Journal,* 1969, *47,* 958–961.

PIERCE, R. M., AND NORRELL, G. "White Tutors for Black Students." *The Journal of College Student Personnel.* 1970, *11,* 169–172.

PRUITT, A. S. "Black Poor at White Colleges—Personal Growth Goals." *The Journal of College Student Personnel,* 1970, *11,* 3–7.

ROBINSON, A. L., FOSTER, C. C., AND OGILVIE, D. H. (Eds.) *Black Studies in the University.* New Haven: Yale University Press, 1969.

ROBINSON, F. P. "Counseling Psychology Since the Northwestern Conference." In THOMPSON, A. S., AND SUPER, D. E. (Eds.) *The Professional Preparation of Counseling Psychologists.* New York: Teachers College Bureau of Publications, 1964.

ROGERS, C. R. *Counseling and Psychotherapy.* Boston: Houghton Mifflin, 1942.

ROGERS, C. R. *Freedom to Learn.* Columbus, Ohio: Merrill, 1969.

ROGERS, C. R. *Client Centered Therapy.* Boston: Houghton Mifflin, 1951.

ROTH, R. M., HERSHENSON, D. B., AND HILLIARD, T. (Eds.) *The Psychology of Vocational Development.* Boston: Allyn and Bacon, 1970.

SAMLER, J. "Where do Counseling Psychologists Work? What Do They Do? What Should They Do?" In THOMPSON, A. S., AND SUPER, D. E. (Eds.) *The Professional Preparation of Counseling Psychologists.* New York: Teachers College Bureau of Publications, 1964.

SANFORD, N. *Where Colleges Fail: A Study of the Student as a Person.* San Francisco: Jossey-Bass, 1967.

SEEMAN, J. *The Case of Jim.* Nashville: Educational Tests Bureau, 1957.

SHOBEN, E. J., JR. "The College, Psychological Clinics, and Psychological Knowledge." *Journal of Counseling Psychology,* 1956, *3,* 200–205.

SHOBEN, E. J., JR. Editorial, *Journal of Counseling Psychology,* 1958, *5*(2), 82.

SIEGEL, M. *The Counseling of College Students.* New York: The Free Press, 1968.

SILVERMAN, R. J. "The Student Personnel Worker on the Boundary." *The Journal of College Student Personnel,* 1971, *12*(1), 3–6.

SINNETT, E. R., AND DANSKIN, D. G. "Intake and Walk-In Procedure in a College Counseling Setting." *Personnel and Guidance Journal,* 1967, *45,* 445–451.

SMITH, P. M. (Ed.) "Special Issue: What Guidance for Blacks?" *The Personnel and Guidance Journal,* 1970, *48,* 707–766.

SORENSON, G. "Pterodactyls, Passenger Pigeons, and Personnel Workers." *The Personnel and Guidance Journal,* 1965, *43,* 430–437.

TOWNSEND, R. *Up the Organization.* Greenwich, Conn.: Fawcett, 1970.

TRUAX, D. "Focus on Feminine Ferment." *The Journal of College Student Personnel,* 1970, *11,* 323–331.

TYLER, L. E. *The Work of the Counselor* (2nd Ed.) New York: Appleton-Century-Crofts, 1961.

Bibliography

WARMAN, R. E. "The Counseling Role of College and University Counseling Centers." *Journal of Counseling Psychology*, 1961, *8*, 231–237.

WARNATH, C. F. "Ethics, Training, Research: Some Problems for the Counseling Psychologist in an Institutional Setting." *Journal of Counseling Psychology*, 1956, *3*, 280–285.

WARNATH, C. F. College Counseling Center Staff Survey. Mimeographed, Oregon State University, 1970.

WESTLEY, W. A., AND EPSTEIN, N. B. *The Silent Majority: Families of Emotionally Healthy College Students*. San Francisco: Jossey-Bass, 1969.

WILLIAMSON, E. G. *Student Personnel in Colleges and Universities*. New York: McGraw-Hill, 1961.

Index

A

Abortion and counselor, 58–62
ALBERT, G., 16
Alienation among students, 81–82
American Personnel and Guidance Association, 46
American Psychological Association: and approval of programs and internships, questions raised about, 75–76; Division of Counseling, 1; Education and Training Board, counseling programs approved by, 67–68

B

BERENSON, B. G., 67
BISNO, H., 17, 101
Budget problems, 10–11

C

CARKHUFF, R. R., 67
Case records, 32–33
CLARK, D. D., 16

Clerical staff and professional staff, causes of friction between, 32–35
Client-counselor relationships outside counseling room, 35–36
Clinical model, limitations of, 71
Clinical-psychiatric aspects of counseling, 7–8
College counseling. *See* Counseling
College counseling Center Data Bank survey (1970), 25–26; responses to questions on, 134–162
Colleges, beginnings of counseling centers in, 3–6
Counseling: as clinical-psychiatric service, 7–8; current status of, 6–7; development of, 3–6; educational-vocational aspects of, 6–7, 13–14; limitations of clinical model, of, 71; limitations of remedial work of, 71; literature on, 16–17; in residence halls, 124–126; trainees

169

in, 8–9, 23; and Veterans Administration guidance bureaus, 3–4; vocational (*see* Vocational counseling)

Counseling Center Data Bank (1970), 25–26; responses to survey questions of, 134–162

Counseling centers: amount of individual counseling in, 10–11, 14–15 (*see also* Individual counseling); budget problems of, 10–11; and campus image, 64; as center for human resources, 114–133; clerical-professional staff friction in, 32–35; directors of, 5–6; doctorate holders in, 67–68; evaluation of, 57–62, 127–133; and faculty, 121–123, 129–130; and freshman programs, 52–53; and group counseling, 51; "hidden need" effect of, 59; and job assignments, 38–39; and leadership training courses, 123–124; and marriage problems of students, 61; and needs of students, 57–62, 116–120; procedures for handling cases in, 30–31; "professional standards" syndrome in, 66–68; psychiatric consultant in, 39; retention function of, 12–13; staff contacts with directors in, 37; student resistance to, 57–58, 60, 64; trainee programs for, 8–9, 23; and vocational counseling, 53, 77–93 (*see also* Vocational counseling)

Counseling centers, comparative survey of: academic advising in, 22; activities and services of, 21–24; administration of national testing programs in, 23–24; and counseling load, 20–21; counselors' roles in, 25–26;

directors of, 19–21; and drop-in or instant intake, 24–25; guidance-oriented, 21–22; location of on campus, 18–19; staff orientations and types of service in, 21–24; therapeutically oriented, 21; use of doctoral interns in, 23

Counseling psychologists. *See* Counselor(s)

Counselor(s): active involvement of on campus, 54–56, 115–117; administrative and professional limitations on activities of, 27–32; and clerical staff, problems with, 32–35; communcation skills of, 115–116; in crisis situations, 60–61; vs. deans of students, 41–44, 105–106, 130–132; disassociation of from power structure, 39–40, 42–44, 53–54; doctoral-level, 69–72; early, 5–6; and minority students, 14, 87–90, 92; new roles of, 46–62; problems of, 1–15; as psychometrists, 85; relations of with faculty, 39–41, 121–123, 129–130; relations of with professional colleagues, 36–39; relations of with staff psychiatrist, 39; roles of, 11–12, 25–26, 46–62; social involvement of with clients, 35–36; and student explosion, 61–62, 117–119; and student personnel workers, 41–44, 105–106, 130–132; training of (*see* Training programs); and use of potential resource people, 66

Counselor-client relationships outside counseling room, 35–36

D

DANSKIN, D. G., 16, 24, 120, 125, 126, 128

Index

Data Bank survey (Magoon), 25–26; responses to questions of, 134–162

Deans of students, 95; vs. counselors, 41–44, 108, 130–132; and fraternity-sorority system, 110–111; managerial-business aspects of job of, 100–101, 103–104; relations of with students, 102; students' image of, 108–111, 112–113; weakened position of on campus, 99–101, 106–107. *See also* Student personnel workers

DEMOS, G. D., 16

Directors of counseling centers, 19–21; counseling load of, 20–21; staff contact with, 37

Doctorate requirement, 67–68; contradictions in, 69–71

Draft resistance and counselor, 58–62

Drop-in clients, 24–25

Drop-outs, freshman, 52–53

Drugs and counselor, 58–62

E

Educational-vocational aspects of counseling, 6–7, 13–14

Ethnic minorities and vocational counseling, 87–90, 92

Evaluation of program, 127–133

F

Faculty and counseling center, 39–41, 121–123, 129–130

Faculty-student relationships, 122–123

Fraternity-sorority system, 110–111

Freshman programs, 52–53

G

GALLAGHER, P. J., 16

GORDON, J. E., 60

Group counseling, 51

H

HALLECK, S. L., 14

"Hidden need" effect, 59

HODGKINSON, H. H., 100

I

Individual counseling, 10–11, 14–15, 63, 64–65; administrative reactions against, 56, 65; faculty attitudes toward, 65; and inadequate staff and time, 49–51; one-contact cases in, 50; and "professional standards" syndrome, 66–68

Internships, 28–29, 76. *See also* Training programs

IVEY, A. E., 19, 20, 21, 67, 68

K

KIRK, B., 17

KOILE, E. A., 16

L

Leadership training courses, 123–124

M

MC LEAN, P. E., 19

MAGOON, T. M., 10, 25, 26

Magoon's Data Bank survey, 25–26; responses to questions on, 134–162

Marriage problems of students, 61

Minority groups, vocational counseling of, 14, 87–90, 92

MUELLER, K. H., 12, 16

N

NDEA, 85, 87, 92

O

OETTING, E. R., 19, 20, 21, 67, 68

One-to-one counseling. *See* Individual counseling

171

Index